THE PROFILE OF COMMUNISM

Revised and edited by

M O S H E D E C T E R

THE

OF

PROFILE COMMUNISM:

A Fact-by-Fact Primer

COLLIER BOOKS

NEW YORK, N.Y.

Contents

6 / Contents

8 / Contents

Part Two / Communist Rule   105

1 THE SOVIET EMPIRE   107

2 TOTALITARIAN NATURE OF THE SOVIET WORLD   116

It has been alleged that the Soviet Union advances the principle of peaceful coexistence merely out of tactical considerations. . . . Yet it is common knowledge that we have always, from the very first years of Soviet power, stood with equal firmness for peaceful coexistence. Hence it is not a tactical move, but a fundamental principle of Soviet foreign policy.

—*Nikita S. Khrushchev, at the 20th Congress of the Soviet Communist Party, Moscow, February 1956.*

We must realize that we [the Communist world and the West] cannot coexist eternally, for a long time. One of us must go to the grave. We do not want to go to the grave. They do not want to go to their grave either. So what can be done? We must push them to their grave.

—*Nikita S. Khrushchev, at a Polish Communist Party meeting in Warsaw, April 1955.*

FOREWORD

THIS IS a primer on communism.

As with scores of books, tracts and articles in which the printed word is serving freedom's cause in the present ideological conflict, this pamphlet is enlisted in the cause of American democracy.

But why a primer, a book of definitions?

It is an uncomfortable truth that the intensity and volubility which characterize our approach to the problems posed by communism—is there a more sustained topic in the press or on television, in the halls of Congress or at our dinner tables?—are exceeded only by the weight of ignorance, misinformation and wishful thinking surrounding it.

America, and the free world which it leads, faces today and for the foreseeable future an unprecedented challenge to its free institutions, security and growth. That challenge stems from the rise to power of communist regimes in Russia, China and their satellites.

It matters a great deal, then, in coping with the challenge, to know which of the above statements by Soviet Premier Khrushchev—both of which he has repeated endless times in one form or another—represents the true face of the communist challenge. This primer hopes to meet that need.

The communist challenge to the free nations, and to the fledgeling nations emerging from colonialism in Africa and Asia, is posed on many fronts at once—military, economic, political and ideological. It is a challenge that can be adequately met only through proper understanding, steady nerves, and a spirit of greatness.

Not enough Americans have a "working" knowledge of communism's features and characteristics and of its historical background. This is an unwholesome situation, for it is precisely this knowledge which is indispensable to meet the challenge; to fend off, on the one hand, the attempts of opportunists, demagogues and bigots to exploit fears based on ignorance, and, on the other hand, the siren songs of the communist appeals on the international scene.

At home, extremists try to mislead the nation into believing that American patriotism consists solely of hatred of communism. We must fight communism, yes; but we must also love democracy more. The Bill of Rights and the Constitution were too dearly won to be surrendered to the Trojan Horses of totalitarianism.

Free men, at home and abroad, will not be able to cope with the communist challenge and threat unless they are aware of its theory and history. What are its principles? What are its objectives? What is its mode of operation? What is its historical record? And what of the language it speaks, and the meaning of its own brand of semantics? How many Americans comprehend —and how many more are bewildered—when a communist leader speaks of such things as "peaceful coexistence"?

The Anti-Defamation League of B'nai B'rith, as an organization dedicated to the American ideal and to the continuing security and welfare of the Jewish community in America, has long recognized the incompatibility of communism with the moral concepts of Judaism and the political concepts of democratic America. Hence, our sponsorship of this pamphlet. It presents no formulae, interprets no theories, argues no briefs. It deals in facts. And it is presented to the learner (it was written for those who want to learn, not read) in question and answer form.

Because the League's objective in presenting *The Profile of Communism,* as well as its earlier versions, has been an educational one, we are pleased that the Crowell-Collier Publishing Company has undertaken to publish this latest revised edition and to bring it to the attention of a wider public. We are indebted to Mr. Moshe Decter, author, long-time student of Communism and former Managing Editor of *The New Leader* magazine, who revised and edited this publication. We are also grateful to Frank N. Trager, who originated the idea for this book, and to Dr. Joseph L. Lichten and Mr. Oscar Cohen of the Anti-Defamation League, under whose supervision this book was prepared.

BENJAMIN R. EPSTEIN
National Director
Anti-Defamation League
of B'nai B'rith

Chapter 1

The Communist Program

What Is Communism?

IT IS an integrated, centralized, world-wide movement, motivated by the Marxist-Leninist ideology, propelled by the apparatus of the supranational Communist Party, abetted by the Party's auxiliaries, powered and directed by the ruling hierarchy of the Communist Party and dictatorial government of the Union of Soviet Socialist Republics.

What Is the Objective of the Communist Movement?

According to communist ideology, the communist movement has a double objective: to destroy all democratic and other non-communist governmental systems and ways of life and to replace them with the universal rule of the communist system, under the leadership of the U.S.S.R.

What Is the Function of the Communist Party?

Again according to communist ideology, the forces of history are working toward the inevitable collapse of capitalism throughout the world and the revolutionary triumph of the international proletariat. The function of the communist party, which is proclaimed as the "vanguard party of the working class," is to hasten the historical process by leading the proletariat to its triumph.

What Is the Role of the Soviet Union in the International Communist Movement?

Since the Bolshevik Revolution in Russia in 1917, the Soviet Union has come to occupy a unique position in communist ideology, strategy and tactics. As the first, and still the most powerful, communist state in the world, the

19

U.S.S.R. became the embodiment of communist mystique and prestige, the source of tangible power and material means, the shrine of unquestioned authority in theory and practice, the model of a successful revolutionary communist party and government.

For the communist party member, then, the achievement of communist objectives has long since become indistinguishable from the advancement of the U.S.S.R.'s interests and power throughout the world. This transformation is most clearly reflected by the fact that the communist party's accession to power—whether in Russia, China or their satellites—has invariably been accompanied not by the triumph of the working class, but by the subjugation of the working class (and all other elements of the population) to the monolithic, totalitarian and terrorist rule of the party.

By the same token, the party's function has been transformed into that of a professional apparatus which uses every conceivable legal and illegal tactic and technique in the service of Soviet power and policy.

Is Communism a Soviet Invention?

No. The term "communism" was coined in the 1830s in the secret revolutionary societies of Paris. Originally, it meant the belief in, and practice of, common ownership, use and disposition of property.

In that sense, communism signified a protest against existing social evils and injustice. It represented an ancient religious and utopian ideal of a social system free of economic and social inequality and political oppression. In that sense, too, it is synonymous with socialism, a term also coined *before* Marx, in 1827 in the Owenite *Co-operative Magazine*. This term was used at first to describe the beliefs and experiments of the idealistic social reformers, Robert Owen, François Fourier and Claude Saint-Simon among others.

But communism did not long remain an eloquent protest and visionary social ideal. It acquired a systematic program and a flexible strategy. It became organized as a world-wide revolutionary movement. And it culminated finally in a new, odious, totalitarian social system embodied first in the Union of Soviet Socialist Republics, subsequently in the empire created by the Soviet Union in Europe, and finally in China and its satellites in Asia. The specter of militant, aggressive Soviet communism now haunts the world.

Who Formulated the Basic Doctrines of Modern Communism?

Until Marx's death the basic doctrines of modern communism were formulated by Karl Marx and Frederick Engels in collaboration, and then by Engels alone until his own death late in the nineteenth century. To distinguish their ideas from those of their utopian socialist predecessors and contemporaries, Marx and Engels called their theories "scientific" socialism. But "scientific" socialism, to them, meant communism, and the first organization they founded was named the Communist League. Its declaration of aims was stated in the *Communist Manifesto*.

In addition to Marxism (so called because Marx is considered to have contributed more significantly than Engels to the formulation), others have helped shape the basic doctrines of modern communism. Among these later contributions, the most important were made by the founder of the Soviet state in Russia, Vladimir Ilyitch Ulyanov, known as Lenin. Lenin's theoretical ideas, as explicated in a multitude of books, pamphlets, editorials and speeches that he poured forth in the quarter-century from 1898 until his death in 1924, are called Leninism. And the entire body of communist doctrine is now customarily called Marxism-Leninism.

During Joseph Stalin's dictatorship, from 1924 until his death in 1953—and especially after his firm consolidation of power in 1928—the few doctrinal ideas he advanced were added to the communist canon, and the whole was designated Marxism-Leninism-Stalinism.

Since Stalin's death, and especially since his official downgrading in the "secret report" (still unpublished in the U.S.S.R. today) given by Premier Khrushchev to the

20th Soviet Communist Party Congress in February 1956, Stalin is referred to, if at all, not as a theoretician, but as a "builder" of communism, who contributed much to the growth of Soviet power but who also committed many "errors" as a result of his "cult of personality." The name of the doctrine has now reverted to "Marxism-Leninism."

Khrushchev himself has introduced no doctrinal innovations, though he has greatly enhanced and expanded the flexibility and range of application of traditional communist strategy and tactics. He constantly reiterates his devotion to "Leninist principles."

What Is Marxism?

The theory of Marxism comprises four principal doctrines: the theories of "historical materialism," "dialectical materialism," "surplus value," and the "class struggle."

What Is Historical Materialism?

The materialist conception of history, generally called "historical materialism," holds that the nature of the political institutions and intellectual life of society are determined by the economic forces which are their foundation. And the history of civilization, in the Marxist view is, primarily, a series of social systems—Asiatic society, chattel slavery, feudalism, capitalism—each based on a particular method of exploitation of labor and each divided into exploiting and exploited, ruling and opposed classes.

What Is Dialectical Materialism?

Dialectical materialism is the communists' term for their theory of social change. It comes from a concept adapted from a German philosopher, Hegel.

According to dialectical materialism, every force in the life of a society brings into existence an opposing force. From the inevitable clash between the two, results a third force combining elements of both original forces. In this way, Marx believed that capitalism produces within itself the seeds of its own destruction—revolt among its workers—and that out of this conflict would come eventually a new force, the communist society.

What Is the Theory of Surplus Value?

According to this theory, 1) labor is the sole creator of value; 2) the wages labor receives represent less than the total value it creates; and 3) the value created by labor in excess of its wages (i.e., the surplus value) is appropriated by the capitalist who thereby exploits labor. This, according to Marxism, accounts for the major inequalities and evils of capitalist society.

What Is the Theory of the Class Struggle?

"The history of all human society, that is all written history, past and present," declares the *Communist Manifesto,* "has been the history of class struggles."

The class struggle is a "perpetual warfare" which is "sometimes masked" and "sometimes open and acknowledged," between "oppressor and oppressed," exploiting and exploited classes.

In the past, the class struggle "invariably ended either in a revolutionary change in the whole structure of society, or else in the common ruin of the contending classes."

Marx held that this is bound to happen to capitalist society as well.

What Outcome of the Class Struggle in Capitalist Society Did Marx Foresee?

In his view, the class struggle in a capitalist society would culminate in a proletarian revolution. The revolution would be, ultimately, world-wide in scope and would be violent in nature.

"The communists" says the *Manifesto,* "disdain to conceal their views and aims." They "openly declare that their ends can be attained only by the forcible overthrow of all existing social conditions."

In Marxist theory, the capitalist state is the organized power of the exploiting class. Its functions are 1) the perpetuation of the economic system on which it is founded, and 2) the suppression of the exploited class. Regardless of its form, Marxism holds, whether monarchy, republic, or corporate state, the capitalist state is a dictatorship of the capitalist class over the working class.

Such being the case, the working class, said Marx, cannot use "the available ready machinery of the state and set it going for its own ends." The working class must seize power through revolution, smash the capitalist state, and crush the resistance of the capitalists. Then, "organized as the ruling class," it can proceed to the eventual building of a communist society.

In 1872 Marx modified his original position by admitting that peaceful transition from capitalism to socialism might take place in England, the United States, and perhaps Holland.

What Was Marx's View of Communist Society?

Marx believed that in a communist society the means of production and exchange would be socially owned and the exploitation of man by man would be eliminated. Hence, the state and all forms of political coercion would be unnecessary and non-existent. The character of man would be transformed through the elimination of self-interest as the primary motive of social conduct and through the free development of individual human personality based on the principle "from each according to his ability, to each according to his needs." Thereby would be opened a new and fruitful epoch in the progress of humanity. The earlier or "lower phase" of the future society, in which economic inequality and the state would still exist, Marx called "socialism."

What Is the Theory of the Dictatorship of the Proletariat?

"Between the capitalist and communist systems of society," Marx wrote in 1875, "lies the period of the revolutionary transformation of the one into the other. This corresponds to a political transition period whose state can be nothing else but the revolutionary dictatorship of the proletariat."

By "dictatorship of the proletariat," he meant a dictatorship of the working class over the defeated capitalists, landlords, and other "exploiters." Like other seers he was vague about when his prophecy would be fulfilled. He did not predict how long the transformation from capitalism to communism would take, nor how long the dictatorship of the proletariat would last. But he thought that as socialism was realized the need for the state would disappear and it would "wither away."

Do All Socialists Accept Marx's Views?

No. Beginning in the 1890s, another current of ideas became predominant in the thinking of socialists. The central doctrine of this current, known as "revisionism" because of the revision of Marx's ideas on which it was based, held that the working class could achieve its rightful place by peaceful means—through elections—and construct socialism gradually and democratically. These ideas became the cornerstone of democratic socialism as distinguished from communism.

The best-known non-Marxist application of these ideas took place in England, following the victory of the Labor Party in the general election of 1945. There, as in several other West European, Scandinavian and Asian countries, democratic socialism has come to be regarded as a constructive force for individual freedom and against all forms of totalitarianism.

What Is Leninism?

Lenin, unlike Marx, was neither an original scholar nor a philosopher of history. His genius lay in the field of political action, in the application of Marxist analytical categories and doctrines to the paramount problem of seizing, maintaining and extending revolutionary power.

In the process, he developed, modified, and more often than not, drastically revised the structure of Marx's ideas. Thus, Lenin agreed with major Marxist doctrines: the total rejection of present-day society, the inevitability, totality and irreconcilability of the class struggle, and the dictatorship of the proletariat.

But whereas for Marx these ideas were primarily intellectual categories for understanding the processes of history or predictions based on his analysis of history—in Lenin's hands they were transformed into instruments for achieving political power.

What Were Lenin's Chief Innovations?

Lenin did not by any means confine himself to adapting Marx's theoretical ideas. He was, after all, the creator of the first successful revolutionary communist party, and thus the founder of the Soviet state. All his theoretical innovations must be seen in the context of his work as an organizer and tactician in order to be understood. His major contributions are extensions of or departures from Marx's ideas on: the nature of capitalism, the nature of the revolutionary party, the tactics that the party should use, and the dictatorship of the proletariat.

How Did Lenin View Capitalism?

Lenin had to adjust Marx's prediction about the ultimate development of capitalism to new circumstances. For the fact was that, contrary to Marx's expectations, the workers' standard of living under capitalism steadily improved, and the tensions between capital and labor were somewhat ameliorated.

Lenin's answer, however, was not to regard Marx's analysis as unrealistic and to revise the doctrine accordingly, as was being done, for example, by such Western Marxist theoreticians as Eduard Bernstein and Karl Kautsky. Lenin's hostility to capitalism was, if anything, even more implacable than was that of Marx. He merely filled the old structure with new content.

Thus, his fundamental point was that since Marx's time capitalism had evolved to a higher stage—in fact, its last stage of development. Instead of an economic system controlled by huge industries and powerful industrialists, he saw capitalism as a system run by financial forces which, in turn, controlled the industries and industrialists. Moreover, this higher form of capitalism was no longer characterized by competition between industrial interests, but by monopolistic control of financial interests.

This analysis is intimately associated with Lenin's doctrine of imperialism, which is as relevant today as when he first formulated it in 1916.

What Was Lenin's Theory of Imperialism?

The real motor power of capitalism, according to Lenin, is no longer, as Marx thought, merely the need of capitalists to compete with each other in the domestic market and necessarily to exploit the working class in the process. It is the need of the financial and banker monopolists to obtain new markets outside their countries, to export excess capital to those markets, to control them exclusively, and, in the process, to exploit the resources and labor of colonial countries. Through such exploitation the greatest profits are to be gained. Out of these profits, made at the expense of the colonial peoples, a portion of the working class in the industrialized countries get a share—which explains, at one stroke, why the workers' lot has improved and why their revolutionary zeal has been dimmed. This whole process Lenin called imperialism.

But imperialism leads to severe competition between international monopolies and cartels, and between the governments associated with them, for such markets. It is this competition that leads to a struggle among the world powers, culminating in wars. As Lenin saw it, the struggle had reached an apocalyptic climax; there was nothing left for the imperialists but to fight with growing violence over the division and redivision of the world's resources. This is the highest, and last phase of capitalism, setting the stage for the victorious emergence of a new era in historical development—revolutionary socialism.

What Is the Relevance of
Lenin's Theory of Imperialism Today?

This doctrine laid the groundwork for the total protracted struggle for power of the communist movement on the national and international levels at once. Thus, the "exploiters" are not just the factory owners, but all the rich countries; the "exploited" are not just the majority of workers in advanced countries, but the colonial peoples;

and the class struggle is not merely restricted to the domestic conflict between capital and proletariat, but between exploiters and exploited on the international scene.

Thus, the socialist revolution need not necessarily take place first, as Marx had held, only in the most advanced countries. On the contrary, it can as well, or better, occur in backward countries.

It is this thesis that provided the theoretical foundation for Lenin's successful conquest of power in backward Russia, which served as a guiding line for the communist revolution in China, and which today points the way for communist activists in Asia, Africa and Latin America.

How Did Lenin Conceive of a Revolutionary Party?

Lenin took over and transformed Marx's idea of a revolutionary party as the "vanguard of the working class." But whereas Marx believed that the majority of the proletariat would spontaneously come to follow the leadership of the party toward the revolution and socialism, Lenin asserted that the proletariat could not be relied on to develop revolutionary class-consciousness spontaneously. For, left to its spontaneous feelings, the proletariat would tend to fall back into the inertia of old habits of thought and action and would rest content with minor reforms and gains. To make the revolution, he held, the proletariat had to be won over and led by a vanguard party that was fully conscious of its role, tasks and objectives.

Such a conscious party could only and always be a tight-knit minority, a combat organization of full-time professional revolutionists—people devoting themselves wholly, under centralized control and para-military discipline, in the struggle to overthrow capitalism and construct socialism. This was the kind of party Lenin created to make the revolution, the party whose secret, conspiratorial and disciplined nature was brought to fulfillment by Stalin, and perpetuated by Khrushchev. It was equally the kind of party which the Soviet leadership ceaselessly molded in every other country.

What Was Lenin's Prescription for the Party's Tactics?

Lenin believed that the ultimate, inevitable triumph of communism would be preceded by "protracted conflict," first against the capitalist world, then against all other dissidents. Nevertheless, he realized that for a long time the party would be a weak minority, isolated and impotent to make the revolution unless it sought allies from among the "class enemies." These could be found, depending on the circumstances, among the peasants, the intellectuals or the petty bourgeoisie.

The allies could not, of course, be trusted, nor could the alliances last long; they were to be used for as long as the situation required, and then discarded. The party must feel free to use both legal and illegal means, and to operate both underground and overtly. And one of the key tactics was to be the infiltration and exploitation of every conceivable non-communist institution, group or association, which is to be transformed into a "transmission belt" of communist ideas and objectives.

The purpose of an alliance with a "class enemy" is to isolate and destroy another enemy who is even stronger. When that task is accomplished, another alliance is made so as to isolate and destroy the erstwhile ally—and so on until every enemy force has been eliminated. This tactic, perfected by Stalin, was once graphically described by one of his most rigid and ruthless followers, Matyas Rakosi, former communist dictator of Hungary: "The opposition is to be destroyed by tactics resembling the slicing of a salami."

How Did Lenin Foresee the Dictatorship of the Proletariat?

Where Marx had been rather unspecific about the revolution, the transition from socialism to communism—he believed the revolution would be brought about in one enormous apocalyptic sweep, to be followed by a vague period of transition to communism under the dictatorship of the proletariat, culminating in the "withering away of the state"—Lenin was much more precise.

He realized that the achievement of communism involved a protracted conflict, with advances and retreats, victories and defeats, and that the party's struggle must be waged incessantly even after the triumph of the revolution and the achievement of socialism. For even under socialism, there would remain powerful residues of non-communist classes that were to be destroyed, along with old habits of thought—and this too is to be part of the protracted conflict to be conducted under the dictatorship of the proletariat.

Thus, so long as there remained a country outside the socialist domain, so long as backward and colonial peoples had not attained the level of the socialist state, so long, indeed, that residues of older patterns of thought and action persisted even inside a socialist state—the state would not wither away. On the contrary, the dictatorship of the proletariat would be even more necessary than ever, and it must conduct its conflict with the internal and external enemies, using ruthless force, terror and lawlessness. Thus Lenin wrote:

"The proletariat needs state power, the centralized organization of force, the organization of violence . . . in the work of organizing socialist economy. . . . The dictatorship of the proletariat is the rule—unrestricted by law and based on force—of the proletariat over the bourgeoisie."

Lenin's revolutionary doctrine conceives of the dictatorship of the proletariat as covering the entire "period of transition from capitalism to communism . . . the period of the overthrow and complete abolition of the bourgeoisie." Since by "bourgeoisie" he meant not only capitalists but every dissident element—including workers and even Marxists who disagree with his doctrine—and since "complete abolition" also applies to the "force of habit of millions and tens of millions"—he concluded that the "period of transition" during which the dictatorship of the proletariat must prevail ". . . inevitably becomes a period of unusually violent class struggles in their sharpest possible forms. . . ."

What Theoretical Contributions Did Stalin Formulate?

In the fundamentals of communist doctrine, Stalin was an orthodox Marxist and Leninist. His theoretical contributions consisted wholly of adaptations of Lenin's ideas to the situations he confronted. This is true of his doctrine of "socialism in one country," of his conception of the dictatorship of the proletariat, and of his view of the relation of the Soviet Union to the rest of the world.

Just as Lenin was the creator of all the ideas and institutions characteristic of the Soviet regime and of the international communist movement which it leads, so Stalin was the man who brought them all to fruition.

What Is the Theory of Socialism in One Country?

This theory, projected in 1924, after a whole series of revolutions in Europe had been defeated, asserts that the construction of socialist society in a single country is possible.

"We can build socialism," Stalin wrote ". . . for we possess . . . all the requisites for the building of a complete socialist society by. . . our own efforts."

But like his master, Lenin, Stalin saw the U.S.S.R. as encircled by hostile capitalist states awaiting a favorable opportunity to attack it. Should an attack materialize, it would, of course, prevent the construction of a socialist society.

Therefore, Stalin held that for the "final victory of socialism," there was necessary a "complete guarantee against attempted intervention and restoration of capitalism" in the U.S.S.R. And this could be achieved only by the support of the Soviet Union by the "workers of all countries, and still more the victory of these workers in at least several countries. . . ."

It should be stressed that the Soviet use of the word "socialism" is a complete distortion of its true meaning. As used by the Soviets, the word represents a system of repression of individual rights and liberties, a totalitarian managerial state that is the very opposite of socialism. That was the system Stalin had in mind with his theory of "socialism in one country," and that is what contemporary Soviet doctrine means when it calls the U.S.S.R. a "socialist" country today.

True socialism, on the other hand, as it is viewed, for example, by the British Labor Party and by the socialist parties of Scandinavia, Western Europe, the United States, and India, is profoundly committed to democracy, and to the civil, political and economic rights of the individual.

What Was Stalin's Conception of the Dictatorship of the Proletariat?

This doctrine, like that of socialism in one country, is actually only the further application of Lenin's ideas. Like Lenin, Stalin accepted the Marxist theory of the dictatorship of the proletariat, but he followed Lenin's revision of the doctrine that as socialism comes into being the state will wither away.

The Stalin constitution of the Union of Soviet Socialist Republics, adopted in 1936, proclaimed the achievement of socialism in the Soviet Union. Nevertheless, the state showed no sign of withering. In fact, as was evident in the great purges which were in full swing when the constitution was adopted, the state was a terroristic autocracy.

Stalin tried to explain the difference between Marxist theory and Soviet reality. As long as the Soviet Union is encircled by a hostile capitalist world with aggressive designs on the U.S.S.R., he said, the Soviet state must increase its coercive powers; it will wither away only when the capitalist environment of Soviet society is replaced by a communist environment.

What Is Khrushchev's Contribution to Communist Doctrine?

Khrushchev is commonly credited with proclaiming the doctrine of "peaceful coexistence" and the denial of the inevitability of war between the communist and the noncommunist worlds. Actually, he has only adapted in a skillful and flexible way all the basic doctrines laid down by Lenin and furthered by Stalin. This is the meaning of his constant iteration of his dedication to "Leninist principles."

Thus, Lenin preached the gospel of all-out hostility to the non-communist world:

"We are living not merely in a state, but in a system of states; and it is inconceivable that the Soviet republic should continue to exist for a long period side by side with imperialist states. Ultimately one or the other must conquer. Meanwhile a number of terrible clashes between the Soviet republic and the bourgeois states is inevitable."

Similarly, the Sixth Congress of the Communist International, meeting in Moscow in 1928 after Stalin had fully consolidated his dictatorial power, declared:

"The Soviet Union harbors no illusion as to the possibility of durable peace. . . . Wars of proletarian dictatorship against world capitalism are inevitable and revolutionary. . . ."

No less than Marx, Lenin and Stalin does Khrushchev believe in the inevitable triumph of communism. In 1958, he said:

"It is now becoming more and more clear that the end of the sway of capitalism is drawing near in other countries, too, and that capitalism is a system that has outlived its age and is bound to perish. The future is ours! The future is for Marxism-Leninism! The future is for communism! . . ."

Meanwhile, however, the forces of communism are still not strong enough to take over the whole world. And it is for just such a period as this one that Lenin and Stalin laid down the lines which Khrushchev now follows.

From the beginning of the Soviet state, Lenin applied to its foreign policy the same general principles of revolutionary strategy as he advocated for the party during the period when the party would be a weak minority: it must maintain alliances, agree to a certain amount of tactical cooperation with the enemy, and be prepared to conduct a protracted conflict. This adds up to a doctrine of "peaceful coexistence" in Soviet foreign policy, accompanied by active exploitation of weak spots in the non-communist world. This double line runs through all communist thinking, from Lenin to Stalin to Khrushchev.

Thus Lenin clearly implied the principle of "peaceful coexistence":

"Dictatorship is a state of acute war. We are precisely in such a state . . . Until the final issue is decided, the state of awful war will continue . . . Our point of view is: for the time being—important concessions and the greatest caution, precisely because a certain equilibrium has set in, precisely because we are weaker than our combined enemies . . .

"The proper tactics for the communist to adopt is to utilize these vacillations [of non-communists] and not to ignore them; and utilizing them calls for concessions to those elements which are turning toward the proletariat . . . while simultaneously fighting those who turn toward the bourgeoisie . . .

". . . To accept battle at a time when it is obviously advantageous to the enemy and not to us is a crime; and those political leaders of the revolutionary class who are unable 'to tack, to maneuver, to compromise,' in order to avoid an obviously disadvantageous battle, are good for nothing."

This is how Stalin perpetuated this doctrine:

"We must not forget Lenin's statement that as regards our work of construction very much depends upon whether we succeed in postponing war with the capitalist world, which is inevitable, but which can be postponed either until the moment when the proletarian revolution in Europe matures, or until the moment when the colonial revolutions have fully matured. . . .

"Therefore, the maintenance of peaceful relations with the capitalist countries is an obligatory task for us. Our relations with the capitalist countries are based on the assumption that the coexistence of two opposite systems is possible."

And, Khrushchev elaborates:

". . . The Leninist principle of the peaceful coexistence of states with different social systems has always been and remains the general line of our country's foreign policy.

"It has been alleged that the Soviet Union advances the principle of peaceful coexistence out of tactical considerations, considerations of expediency. Yet it is common knowledge that we have always, from the very first years of Soviet power, stood with equal firmness for peaceful coexistence . . .

"In the countries where capitalism is still strong and has a huge military and police apparatus at its disposal, the reactionary forces will of course inevitably offer serious resistance. There the transition to socialism will be attended by a sharp class, revolutionary struggle . . .

"Leninism teaches us that the ruling classes will not surrender their power voluntarily. And the greater or lesser degree of intensity which the struggle may assume, the use or non-use of violence in the transition to socialism, depends on the resistance of the exploiters . . ."

What Is the Current Blueprint of Communist Strategy and Tactics?

On December 6, 1960, the leaders of 81 communist parties from all over the world, who had been meeting in the Kremlin for exactly one month, issued a lengthy manifesto detailing their consensus on strategy and tactics for the coming period.

On January 6, 1961, Nikita Khrushchev, in a speech to the top representatives of the most important communist party organs inside the U.S.S.R., clarified and expanded upon the manifesto issued the preceding month.

Though none of the ideas in these two documents is exactly new, they represent, in concentrated form, an authoritative portrait of the meaning of peaceful coexistence in the present state of world affairs. Together, these neglected but decisive documents clearly present the guidelines by which the Kremlin and its allies intend to secure the victory of the world communist movement.

The three inter-related keys to the current communist blueprint are: "the world socialist system," "the peace movement," and "the national liberation movement."

What Is the Soviet "Third Program"?

The first program of the Bolshevik Party was adopted at its Second Congress in 1903. This program called on the working class of Russia to fight for the overthrow of the Tsarist autocracy and for the establishment of the dictatorship of the proletariat. The second program, which reflected Lenin's adherence to the theories of Marx, was adopted by the 7th Congress of the Soviet Communist Party in 1919. With this program as its base, the Communists set out to establish a dictatorship in the U.S.S.R.

The third program was prepared by Khrushchev to be presented to the 22nd Congress of the Soviet Communist Party in October 1961. The new manifesto claims that since the tasks of the first two programs have been "carried out" the third program is necessary "for the building of Communist society."

Despite all the quasi-ideological language and tenor of the document, it represents a major political expression of the current attitudes of the Khrushchev government as related to the contemporary problems of the world. On the one hand the program reverses Lenin's (and Mao Tse-Tung's) thesis that war is necessary to destroy capitalism, and states that peaceful co-existence is possible, thus deviating from Marxist principles. On the other hand, it heralds the "triumph of Socialism and Communism on a world-wide scale." It states also that as long as the whole world has not become communist, war is possible, and therefore, the Soviets will continue the build-up of their armed forces. In addition, the document declares that the Soviet Union will be ready militarily, politically, economically and through propaganda means to back its thesis that "socialism will inevitably succeed capitalism everywhere." These inconsistencies of the new program have been viewed by the West as a concession to the Chinese point of view which considers war with non-Communist countries as inevitable.

Among the many promises which the "third manifesto" contains is a pledge to include the people of the Soviet Union in the processes of government (no mention is made, however, of individual freedom and the rule of law), free education, free medical services, free housing, and overtaking the United States in production. All of these promises, however, are qualified by "conditions of peace"—for, as long as the international situation remains complicated, "the resulting necessity of increasing defense expenditures may hold up the fulfillment of the plan." Some observers believe the many escape clauses listed in Khrushchev's plan are indications that the goals of the third program are unrealistic.

What Is the Role of the World Socialist System in the Communist Blueprint?

The "world socialist system," in Moscow's definition, is in fact the world communist movement, which includes the Soviet and Chinese regimes and all their satellites in Europe and Asia (and in Cuba) and the communist parties elsewhere in the world.

As Khrushchev has repeatedly emphasized in many speeches during the past few years, and as the current official blueprint spells out in greater detail—there has now occurred a significant shift in the balance of world forces. This shift is increasingly in favor of the powerful world socialist system. Concomitantly, the "camp of capitalism and imperialism" is increasingly consumed with internal and external crises and is growing ever weaker. Thus the manifesto declares:

"It is the principal characteristic of our time that the world socialist system is becoming the decisive factor in the development of society. . . . Today it is the world socialist system . . . that determines the main content, main trend and main features of the historical development of society. Whatever efforts imperialism makes, it cannot stop the advance of history. A reliable basis has been provided for further decisive victories for socialism. The complete triumph of socialism is inevitable."

It is this faith which is the basis and the source of communist dynamism throughout the world today. The ebullience with which Khrushchev and his cohorts proclaim that the future is theirs is not just a matter of faith, however. Their dynamism is bolstered both by the growing weakness and vacillation of non-communist powers and the technological advances of the U.S.S.R. Whether or not these advances are indeed as great as claimed, they have become an effective instrument in the arsenal of the political-psychological warfare which the Kremlin conducts to persuade non-aligned peoples that the future belongs to communism.

What Is the Role of the Peace
Movement in the Communist Blueprint?

As the manifesto has it, "the peace movement is the broadest movement of our time, involving people of diverse political and religious creeds, of diverse classes of society, who are all united by the noble urge to prevent new wars and to secure enduring peace."

Precisely because the balance of world power is shifting in favor of the world communist movement, the blueprint envisages the likelihood of the revolutionary overthrow of "capitalist imperialism" without a major world war. And the widespread, understandable fear of nuclear holocaust is to be exploited and manipulated as a major instrument with which to render the non-communist world wholly ineffectual. The manifesto defines a fundamental aspect of the policy of peaceful coexistence as "the broadest possible united front of peace supporters, fighters against the imperialist policy of aggression and war inspired by U. S. imperialism."

And Khrushchev defines it as the "maximum utilization of the revolutionary possibilities of the various classes and social strata and for drawing all allies—no matter how inconsistent, shaky and unstable—into the struggle against imperialism."

What Is the Role of National Liberation
Movements in the Communist Blueprint?

The struggle for national independence going on all over the less developed part of the world is one of the two main international phenomena (alongside the universal desire for peace) which the communists seek to subvert, control and manipulate as a weapon against the West. As the manifesto puts it: "The complete collapse of colonialism is imminent. The breakdown of the system of colonial slavery under the impact of the national liberation movement is a development ranking second in historic importance only to the formation of the world socialist system."

The manifesto proclaims the support of world communism for this movement: "All the socialist countries and the international working class and communist movement see it as their duty to render the fullest moral and material assistance to the peoples fighting to free themselves from imperialist and colonial tyranny."

This support was decisively clarified, in fact, by Khrushchev, who declared that it is "an outright lie" that the "national liberation movement can develop independently of the struggle which the working class wages for socialism, and [independently] of support from the socialist countries." In so many words, then, Khrushchev makes it clear that national independence of former colonial peoples is quite meaningless unless it is guided and controlled by the communist movement.

Nowhere, of course, do these documents indicate that it is precisely such "capitalist, imperialist" countries as England and France that have massively liberated their colonies in Asia and Africa—and that today the only colonial powers of significance are the U.S.S.R. and Communist China, who hold hundreds of millions of people in their Asian and East European satellites subject to their tyrannies.

Does Peaceful Coexistence Presage an Ideological Truce?

No. The manifesto is quite explicit on this point:

"Peaceful coexistence of states does not imply renunciation of the class struggle. The coexistence of states with different social systems is a form of class struggle between socialism and capitalism.

"In conditions of peaceful coexistence, favorable opportunities are provided for the development of the class struggle in the capitalist countries and in the national liberation movement of the peoples of the colonial and dependent countries. . . .

"Peaceful coexistence of countries with different social systems does not mean conciliation of the socialist and bourgeois ideologies. On the contrary, it implies intensification of the struggle of the working class, of all the Communist parties, for the triumph of socialist ideas."

A more open and forthright declaration of ideological and political warfare could not be asked for.

Does Peaceful Coexistence Preclude Violence Against Democracies?

No. The Khrushchevian manifesto reiterates the Lenin Stalin doctrine that in a number of capitalist countries the time may soon come when the "working class" (the communist party) may be in a position to seek power through peaceful, legal parliamentary means. But:

"In the event of the exploiting classes' resorting to violence against people, the possibility of *non-peaceful* transition to socialism should be borne in mind. Leninism teaches, and experience confirms, that the ruling classes never relinquish power voluntarily. In this case, the degree of bitterness and the forms of the class struggle will depend not so much on the proletariat as on the resistance put up by the reactionary circles to the will of the overwhelming majority of the people, on these circles' using force at one or another stage of the struggle for socialism."

In other words, no democratic resistance to a communist uprising is legitimate. When the party is ready to opt for a coup, any violence against democratic institutions is legitimate.

Does Peaceful Coexistence Preclude Violence in the National Liberation Movement?

No. The new communist manifesto applies the same rule in the "anti-colonial" struggle as in the anti-democratic struggle:

"The peoples of the colonial countries win their independence both through armed struggle and by non-military means, depending on the specific conditions in the country concerned. They secure durable victory through a powerful national liberation movement. The colonial powers never bestow freedom on the colonial peoples and never leave of their own free will the countries they are exploiting."

This is, in short, a threat and a promise that the communist movement has committed itself to "armed struggle" in behalf of communist-led national liberation movements, which are, by definition, the only ones worthy of the name. In fact, the manifesto goes so far as to justify such armed struggle:

"Communists have always recognized the *progressive,* revolutionary significance of national liberation wars."

And Khrushchev has characteristically dotted the I's and crossed the T's with his flat assertion that "national liberation wars will continue to be inevitable as long as Western imperialism continues to exist."

Who Is the Main Enemy in This Struggle?

"U. S. imperialism is the main force of aggression and war. Its policy embodies the ideology of militant reaction."

So declares the new communist manifesto.

What, Then, Is the Communist Conception of the Relation of the Soviet Union to the Free World?

No clearer blueprint has been provided than the military plan offered by Stalin. It can well be studied alongside Khrushchev's present international diplomacy:

". . . Objective: to consolidate the dictatorship of the proletariat in one country, using it as a base for the defeat of imperialism in all countries . . . The main forces of the revolution: the dictatorship of the proletariat in one country, the revolutionary movement of the proletariat in all countries. Main reserves: the semi-proletarian and small-peasant masses in the developed countries, the liberation movement in the colonies and dependent countries. Direction of the main blow: isolation of the petty-bourgeois democrats, isolation of the parties of the Second International [democratic socialists throughout the world] . . . Plan for the disposition of forces: alliance of the proletarian revolution with the liberation movement in the colonies and the dependent countries."

Bibliography

These are the basic writings of the men who have made communism.

Lenin, V. I.

STATE AND REVOLUTION, International Publishers, 1932.

SELECTED WORKS, 12 vols., International Publishers, 1935.

Mager, N. H., and Katel, Jacques

CONQUEST WITHOUT WAR, Simon and Schuster, 1961.

An invaluable collection, with comment and notes, of Nikita Khrushchev's writings and speeches on the basic issues of East-West relations.

Marx, Karl and Engels, Frederick

THE COMMUNIST MANIFESTO, International Publishers.

Marx, Karl

THE CIVIL WAR IN FRANCE, International Publishers, 1940.

CRITIQUE OF THE GOTHA PROGRAMME, International Publishers, 1933.

Stalin, Joseph

FOUNDATIONS OF LENINISM, International Publishers, 1932.

MARXISM AND THE NATIONAL AND COLONIAL QUESTION, International Publishers.

SHORT HISTORY OF THE COMMUNIST PARTY

OF THE SOVIET UNION (BOLSHEVIKS), International Publishers, 1939.

Trotsky, Leon
THE HISTORY OF THE RUSSIAN REVOLUTION, University of Michigan Press, 1959.
   A massive account by Lenin's most brilliant second-in-command.

The following two volumes are excellent introductory collections.

Feuer, Lewis
MARX AND ENGELS: BASIC WRITINGS ON POLITICS AND PHILOSOPHY, Anchor Books, Doubleday, 1959.
   A basic selection with perceptive analysis by the author.
Hook, Sidney
MARX AND THE MARXISTS, Van Nostrand, 1955.
   A volume of exposition, comment, and readings which can serve as an introduction to the theory and practice of Marxism.

The following books are critical evaluations of Marxist doctrine. They also show the continuing influence of the basic writings on present-day Communist policy.
Fisher, Marguerite
COMMUNIST DOCTRINE AND THE FREE WORLD, Syracuse, 1952.
House of Representatives, 83rd Congress, 1st Session, 1959.
FACTS ON COMMUNISM, VOLUME I: THE COMMUNIST IDEOLOGY.
   A recent study on the subject, written for the House Committee on Un-American Activities by an authority, Professor Gerhart Niemeyer. United States Government Printing Office, Washington, 1959.

Leites, Nathan
A STUDY OF BOLSHEVISM, The Free Press, 1953.
Rossiter, Clinton
MARXISM: THE VIEW FROM AMERICA, Harcourt, Brace & Co., 1960.
> A critical evaluation by a distinguished American political scientist and historian.
Souvarine, Boris
STALIN, Longmans, Green & Co., 1939.
> A pioneering biography, still the best available.
Wetter, Gustav A.
DIALECTICAL MATERIALISM, Praeger, 1959.
> An outstanding scholar explains the basis of Marxist-Leninist ideology.
Wolfe, Bertram D.
KHRUSHCHEV AND STALIN'S GHOST, Praeger, 1957.
> A historical and ideological analysis of Bolshevism, based on a detailed study of Khrushchev's famous "secret speech" of February 1956.

Chapter 2

The Communist Movement

What Kind of Party Is the Communist Party?

ALL COMMUNIST parties are modeled on the Soviet Communist or Bolshevik party, which proclaims itself the only true representative of working class interests and of progress generally. All other parties are, in its view, representatives of anti-working class interests and actually or potentially counter-revolutionary.

What Is Bolshevism?

The term "Bolshevism" is derived from the Russian word for majority. It originated as a convenient epithet to distinguish Lenin's majority group in the Russian Social Democratic Labor Party from his principal opponents who comprised the minority or Menshevik group. Mensheviks opposed communism and favored the ideals of democratic socialism in Russia.

In the course of time, as Lenin's group developed into an independent organization and formulated a distinctive program, and strategy, Bolshevism came to signify the teachings, strategy, tactics, and organizational forms and practices first of Lenin, and after his death, of Stalin.

In a narrow sense, Bolshevism is, therefore, Russian and Soviet communism. In a broader sense, because of the domination of world communism by Lenin and Stalin, Bolshevism is what most people understand today by the simple term "communism."

What Is Trotskyism?

The essential idea in the teachings of Trotsky is the theory of the permanent revolution. This theory, which Trotsky claimed to have derived from certain ideas of Marx and Lenin and which he opposed to Stalin's theory of socialism in one country, rests on three central propositions:

1—"With regard to countries with a belated bourgeois development, especially the colonial and semi-colonial countries . . . democratic and national emancipation is conceivable only through the dictatorship of the proletariat . . ."

2—"The conquest of power by the proletariat" (in any country) "does not terminate the revolution, but only opens it. Socialist construction is conceivable only on the foundation of the class struggle on a national and international scale."

3—"The completion of the socialist revolution within national limits is unthinkable . . . the socialist revolution . . . attains completion only in the final victory of the new society on our entire planet."

At first, Trotsky thought his theory would prevail as the basis of communist doctrine and Soviet policy, and that Stalin would be ousted as a result of a factional struggle within the communist movement. Later, he advocated a political revolution in the Soviet Union to overthrow the Stalinist government. In Soviet propaganda and law, Trotskyism is now another term for fascist, counter-revolutionary thinking and action.

What Is the Relation Between Bolshevism and the Soviet Communist Party?

The Soviet Communist Party is the direct descendant of the Bolshevik, or majority, faction of the Russian Social Democratic Labor Party, created by Lenin in 1903, which later became an independent party. In 1918 it changed its name to the Communist Party. After formation of the Union of Soviet Socialist Republics in 1922, it was renamed Communist Party of the Soviet Union (Bolsheviks).

At the Party's 19th Congress, held in Moscow in 1952, the word "Bolsheviks" in parentheses was dropped and the name it now bears is simply, Communist Party of the Soviet Union.

After the seizure of power in Russia in 1917, the principal function of the Bolshevik party was altered. It now aimed at the organization, direction and administration of the state, the implementation of government policy, and the maintenance of power. In all of these functions, after Lenin's death in 1924, Stalin played the principal role.

In the Soviet Union and other Soviet societies, the communist party is the only legal party. According to the Stalin Constitution of the U.S.S.R., the communist party is "the leading core of all organizations of the working people, both public and state." Communists hold the key positions and communist party units function in virtually all political, economic, military, and cultural institutions and organizations.

How Is the Communist Party Organized?

Structurally, the communist party is a centralized organization based on a caste system. From its base in small cells, units, or branches it rises through intermediate and superior local, district, and regional bodies to its summit in the Central or National Committee. In theory, the Central Committee is the highest authority in the party. In practice it is subordinate to the Presidium, the successor of the famous Politburo.

What Is the Presidium?

Structurally, the Presidium is one of the three fundamental subordinate bodies of the Central Committee of the Soviet Communist Party. The others are the Secretariat and the Party Control Committee.

Nominally, the Presidium directs the work of the Central Committee between plenary sessions. The Secretariat verifies the fulfillment of party decisions and the selections of cadres; and the Party Control Committee supervises the internal policing of the party.

In reality, the Presidium is dominant. Established by the 19th Party Congress, it has assumed the functions of the dissolved Politburo (Political Bureau of the Central Committee of the Party) and of the Orgburo (Organization Bureau of the Central Committee), and it stands at the peak of the party pyramid. Its table of organization calls for ten full members and four alternates, but in fact its policies are determined by a small, unofficial "inner bureau" within the Presidium, whose members wield the ultimate power in the entire international communist movement.

The composition of this inner bureau and of the Presidium has changed several times since Stalin's death. Lavrenti Beria has been shot, Georgi Malenkov, Lazar Kaganovitch, Nikolai Bulganin, V. M. Molotov, Dimitri Shepilov and Mikhail Pervukhin have all been demoted and dispatched to remote parts of the country to assume lowly tasks. And Nikita S. Khrushchev has emerged, if not as the undisputed dictatorial tyrant that Stalin was, clearly as the single most powerful and decisive figure in the leadership of the party, and thus of the government.

But regardless of changes in its make-up or its name, the directorate of the Soviet Communist Party is the seat of ultimate power in Soviet Russia. All organs of the party and the state, including the secret service, the army and bureaucracy are under its complete domination.

What Is Democratic Centralism?

In communist theory, "democratic centralism" is a combination of centralized authority and discipline with democratic practices in the life of the communist party. Theoretically, party policy is decided in free discussion by the membership which also elects the leadership. But once a decision is made, it is binding on all members of the party, and once elected, the leadership must be obeyed. In action, discipline is on a military basis. Theoretically, centralized authority and democracy balance each other and are of equal importance.

In practice, authority and discipline are supreme and democracy is non-existent. Policy is decided and changed at will by the leadership. The membership may or may not be consulted. Party congresses and conventions are postponed by the leadership sometimes for years in violation of the party constitution. The Comintern was dissolved by its executive committee without a mandate from the Comintern Congress, nominally the highest body of the Third International.

When held, congresses are sounding boards for the announcement of decisions made by the leadership. Criticism and opposition are not tolerated. The leaders of communist parties outside the Soviet Union are appointed and deposed by decision of the Presidium of the Bolshevik party. The communist party, said Stalin, must be monolithic. It is exactly that.

Who Are the Communists?

"The Communist Party is formed," reads a statement of the Second Congress of the Comintern, held in 1920, "of the best, most intelligent, self-sacrificing and far-seeing workers."

That the communist movement attracts such workers in many countries is a fact. But it is also a fact that where workers are free to leave the movement, the communist party fails to hold them and even repels them by its policy.

Persons of non-working class origin are also included in the membership of the communist parties. But by choice, the communist parties in capitalist countries and in east and central Europe have their strongest roots among the industrial workers. These they regard as the historically destined leaders of the revolution.

In China, however, the Communist Party is now composed of an overwhelming majority of peasants. This despite the fact that when the party was first organized in 1920 it was essentially a party of workers.

The ultimate nature of all communist parties is indicated by the experience of the Soviet Communist Party. In 1928 when the five-year plans were instituted in the U.S.S.R., the membership of the Soviet party consisted of industrial workers (more than 60%), peasants (over 20%), and clerical workers, intellectuals, and persons of non-working class origin other than peasants.

However, by the time of the Nazi invasion of the Soviet Union in 1941, workers were a distinct minority in the Bolshevik Party. Men and women of the social strata created or enlarged by the industrialization and collectivization programs of the preceding years—plant and farm managers, technicians, engineers, government and party functionaries, and military officers—the elite of Soviet society, comprised a large majority of the Communist Party. Once the workers had performed their revolutionary function in seizing power, in fighting the civil war and enduring the rigors of industrialization, they were relegated to a minor role in the party which controlled the state. This has resulted in their present subordinate and subservient role in Soviet society.

Today, manual workers represent only 30% of the total party membership of 8,708,000: exactly half of their proportion in the '20s.

Why Do People Join the Communist Party?

Some people are attracted by communist propaganda about an "ideal" society based on economic and social equality and on brotherhood. Some workers and peasants, unable to detect the red wolf in the sheep's clothing, take the communist party at its face value as a fighter for their immediate interests.

Some people are deceived or deceive themselves into thinking that the communist party will further the cultural, scientific, fraternal, and other causes in which they are interested. More cynical persons see in the large communist movement opportunities for careers.

Inevitably, when those who were induced, persuaded, or enticed into the communist fold discover that they were deceived, they leave. The number of ex-communists is many times greater than the number of party members.

But new recruits are always obtained. The membership rolls fatten on the poverty and misery which constitute the lot of many peoples and races. As long as poverty and misery continue on a large scale, the communist parties will continue to feed on the hopes and aspirations of men to achieve security, freedom, and dignity. As the free world continues to eliminate poverty, and continues to give men hope, it will cut away the ground under communism.

In the Soviet world, people join the communist party because of conviction, hope, indoctrination, a desire or pressure to conform, expediency in getting an education or building a successful career. And also, as the only legal party, it is the only available medium for political life and the realization of political ambition. To quit the communist party in the Soviet world is a risky undertaking.

How Many Communists Are There?

No one knows exactly. The membership of communist parties varies widely. The turnover is large. In addition to those who leave because of disillusionment, large numbers are expelled in the periodic purges which are a prescribed feature of communist party organization.

As of June 1961, statistics published in Moscow (which must be approached with some caution) estimated the membership of 87 communist parties throughout the world at 36,000,000.

Of this number, the vast majority were in the communist bloc of nations. The largest single party was that of China, with more than 15,500,000 members and candidate members. The second largest was that of the Soviet Union, with almost 9,500,000 members and candidate members. More than 4,500,000 members belonged to the communist parties of the Soviet satellites in Eastern Europe—Poland, East Germany, Czechoslovakia, Hungary, Albania, Bulgaria, Rumania.

The same statistics estimate membership in Western Europe (chiefly France and Italy) at 2,500,000, in noncommunist Asian countries at about 2,500,000, in the Western Hemisphere (chiefly Latin America) at over 250,000, and in Africa at 50,000.

It is sobering to learn of the officially claimed increase in membership in Asia and Africa since 1939. In Africa, the number has grown from about 5,000 before World War II to 50,000 today. And in Asia, the number has grown in the corresponding period from around 20,000 to some 2,500,000 *outside* Asian countries ruled by communists.

The Communist party in the United States had reached its historic peak of 75-80,000 members in 1949. By July 1961 the number of party members was variously estimated at between ten and twenty thousand.

Do the 36,000,000 in Communist Parties Constitute the Entire Organized Communist Force?

No. Each communist party has a youth organization and other auxiliaries, many of them larger than the party itself, under its direction.

The Young Communist League of the U.S.S.R., for example, whose members are 15 to 26 years of age, numbers about 18,000,000; and the Young Pioneers, children 9 to 15 years old, numbers about 16,000,000. Altogether the organized, active communist force of the Soviet Union comprises about one-sixth of the population. Similar proportions prevail in Communist China.

In addition to their youth auxiliaries, the parties of the communist bloc of nations, as well as those of France and Italy, also control large and powerful trade union organizations. And all communist parties create auxiliary economic, political, cultural and other civic movements— or seek to infiltrate and subvert non-communist ones— to serve their ends.

Does the Size of a Communist Party Indicate the Danger It Represents?

Not necessarily. Of course, when communist parties are large, they are a greater danger than when they are small. But the fact that they are small does not mean that they are not a potential danger of great importance.

In the United States it is customary to point to the small number of organized communists and dismiss them as an insignificant national force. It is of course true that the Party in this country has, in addition to its tiny numbers, other difficulties which are reflected in the fact that the Party's official organ, the *Daily Worker,* was transformed, for lack of readership support, to a weekly, *The*

Worker. It is also true that the Party has been unable to get on the ballot in New York State, where its largest number of members reside, for lack of supporting primary petitions.

Despite this, it is worthwhile to note an official statement issued in June 1961 by Attorney General Robert Kennedy, immediately after a United States Supreme Court decision ordering the party to register as an agent of the Soviet Union. Mr. Kennedy said:

"After ten years of litigation, the Supreme Court has held that the Communist Party of the United States is directed, dominated and controlled by the Soviet Union. . . . This is a momentous decision. . . . The Communist Party has made every effort to promote a public image of a legitimate political party. . . . In fact, it always has been under the discipline of a foreign country and has been a tactical means of advancing both the short and long-range interests of the Soviet Union.

"It is this point which I believe is of crucial importance. The case and the evidence on this point presented to the Court should be studied by all non-Communist governments and groups, such as teachers, students and labor organizations around the world. What the Communist Party preaches and what it practices is for all to see. . . .

"The Communist Party as it exists in the United States and other countries is not a legitimate political party. . . . It is the Trojan Horse assuming the form of a so-called political party in the democratic countries around the world—agrarian reformers in China, guerrillas in South Vietnam, or rioters in Japan. . . ."

So spoke Attorney General Robert Kennedy.

The fact is that a communist party of *any* size is a serious danger. Any organized, disciplined force with a definite goal and the determination, shrewdness and courage necessary to achieve its ends presents a menace. It is, moreover, a detachment of an international army which commands vast material and human resources upon which it can draw when necessary.

At the outbreak of the Russian Revolution in March,

1917, the Bolshevik Party had only some 40,000 members. One month later, the Bolshevik Party membership doubled. Six months later, the force which organized and led the armed insurrection of October, 1917, numbered only 240,000 in a population larger than the present population of the United States.

After establishment of the Soviet state, the communist parties of the world were able to draw on the enormous resources it commanded.

In June, 1936, one month before the outbreak of the fascist rebellion and the civil war, the Spanish Communist Party had grown from about 150 in 1931 (when the democratic forces overthrew the dictatorship of Primo de Rivera) to about 50,000 members. It was still a minor force compared with the powerful Spanish anarchist and socialist movements. Nevertheless, after the civil war began, the Spanish Communist Party, as a direct result of Soviet pressure on the republican government of Spain, to which it sent limited amounts of aid in cash, became the dominant political force in the republican state. Soviet and Spanish communists were vested with control of the anti-fascist military and police forces of the republic, which they used to establish a reign of terror against anarchists, socialists, and others. They looted the gold reserves of the Bank of Spain and sent them to Moscow. In general they made a major contribution to the defeat of the republican state and the triumph of fascism.

Are Communist Parties Independent and Autonomous?

No. They are directed and controlled by the ruling hierarchy of the Soviet Communist Party in Moscow. This control has, since 1919, assumed various forms, but the degree of control has rarely varied. The first, and perhaps the most famous organ of Moscow's control and direction of the world communist movement was the Third (Communist) International, generally called the Communist International or Comintern.

What Was the Comintern?

From 1919, when it was founded, until 1943, when it was dissolved, the Comintern, created chiefly by Lenin, served as "the general staff of the world revolution."

Its headquarters were situated in Moscow. In theory, the Comintern was independent of the Soviet government. Again, in theory, all affiliated parties of the Comintern were subject to its directives. The Soviet government, controlled by the Soviet Communist Party, was thus at the disposition of the Comintern for purposes of world revolution.

Actually, however, the Comintern was dominated by the Soviet Communist Party and was in fact only an appendage of the latter and, through it, of the Soviet government.

How Was the Communist Movement Directed After 1943?

After the Comintern was dissolved, the coordination and direction of the communist parties was entrusted to the Secret Police of the U.S.S.R. A member of this service was invariably a secret member of the central committee of every party; this is probably still the case today.

In addition, from 1947 to 1955, Moscow's control of the international communist movement was organized through an institution known as the Cominform.

What Was the Cominform?

In 1947, nine European communist parties, including the Soviet, French, and Italian parties, and a number of east and central European parties, established an Information Bureau, since known as the Communist Information Bureau or Cominform. Subsequently, other communist parties affiliated with the Cominform.

Originally, Cominform headquarters was situated in Belgrade, but after the breach between Titoist Yugoslavia and Stalinist Russia in 1948, it was transferred to Bucharest.

The ostensible purpose of the Cominform was "to organize and exchange experience and, in case of necessity, co-ordinate the activity of Communist parties on foundations of mutual agreement."

In reality, the Cominform which, like the Comintern

before it, was dominated by the Soviet Communist Party, was launched as a part of the Soviet Union's retaliation for the Marshall Plan. Its real tasks were:

Consolidation of Soviet power in eastern and central Europe.

Intensification of communist political warfare in western Europe, chiefly through the French and Italian parties.

Creation of an appearance of equality and democracy in relationships among communist parties in the Soviet world.

The Cominform was officially disbanded in April, 1956. Its place has been taken by a variety of formal and informal institutions and organizations. Among these are the Warsaw Pact and the periodic congresses of communist parties of the Soviet bloc. International communist contacts are also maintained through visits to and from Moscow by the Soviet leaders and leaders of other parties in and out of the bloc.

What Is the Warsaw Pact?

The Warsaw Pact is a treaty of "Friendship, Cooperation and Mutual Assistance" concluded in May, 1955, between the governments of the Soviet Union and its seven East European satellites. It is essentially a military pact, offering a show of governmental independence for all the satellites, which formally coordinates the military policies and actions of the Soviet bloc in Europe. It is headed by Soviet Marshal Ivan Konev.

In fact, of course, the Warsaw Pact members are no more independent than were the "autonomous" communist parties that belonged to the Comintern and the Cominform.

The Warsaw Pact has also given rise to formal institutions of economic coordination within the bloc, such as the Council of Mutual Economic Aid. In Stalin's day, this economic coordination, undertaken for the exclusive benefit of the U.S.S.R.'s economy and resulting in enormous exploitation of the resources and labor of the satellites, was simply ordered ruthlessly from Moscow. Since Stalin's death, the worst features of this economic exploitation have been ameliorated; in addition, there is a show of consultation among the various "independent" governments, and a greater degree of rationality in the bloc's total economic planning.

Nevertheless, the satellites still remain subordinate in every field. This is demonstrated by the shift in their economic planning since 1958. In that year, Khrushchev, instead of continuing the traditional five-year plans for Soviet economic development embarked on an ambitious seven-year plan. All the satellites, who had coordinated their own five-year plans with those of the U.S.S.R., fell into line. They terminated their own shorter plans as swiftly as possible and now have adapted their own countries' economic plans to that of the Soviet Union.

Are Communist Parties Really Agencies of the Soviet Government?

Yes. The communist parties always speak in the name of idealistic objectives and of the welfare of the working class and nation in which they function, but their chief purpose and highest duty in peace and war is to serve the interests of the government of the U.S.S.R.

Any service they may render to the working class or to any cause other than their own is for the purpose of advancing their primary aim. According to the situation, they pose as the only true patriots or as the only genuine revolutionary internationalists. Both poses disguise their unchanging subservience to Soviet nationalism and imperialism.

How, for Example, Did the French Communist Party Serve Soviet Interests?

Before Hitler came to power in Germany in January, 1933, the French Communist Party, in common with the German and Soviet governments and with other communist parties, opposed the status quo in Europe created by the Versailles Treaty ending World War I.

In 1935, alarmed by Hitler's victory, the Soviet government made an alliance with France, directed against

Germany. The French Communist Party then became a defender of the status quo.

Following consummation of the Nazi-Soviet alliance in 1939, which provided for the partition of Poland and was the signal for the outbreak of World War II, the French Communist Party opposed the war against Germany as an imperialist war. And after the fall of France in 1940, it collaborated with the German occupation authorities.

But when Germany invaded the Soviet Union in 1941, the French communists became French patriots and entered the resistance movement in force.

During the cold war between the Soviet world and the West, which followed World War II, the French Communist Party fought the Marshall Plan and the shipment of arms from the United States to France.

Bibliography

Almond, Gabriel
THE APPEALS OF COMMUNISM, Princeton University Press, 1954.
> A scholarly investigation into the appeals and vulnerabilities of the communist system.

Borkenau, Franz
EUROPEAN COMMUNISM, Harper, 1953.
> An exhaustive description of European communism as seen by an exceptionally astute observer.

Brzezinski, Z. K.
THE PERMANENT PURGE, Harvard University Press, 1956.
> The strategic role of purges in maintaining communist party discipline and control.

Daniels, Robert Vincent
CONSCIENCE OF THE REVOLUTION, Harvard University Press, 1960.

Graphic portrayal of the fate of opposition groups inside the Communist movement of the U.S.S.R.

Fainsod, Merle
HOW RUSSIA IS RULED, Harvard University Press, 1954.
Analyzes the anatomy of Soviet totalitarianism.

Fainsod, Merle
SMOLENSK UNDER SOVIET RULE, Harvard University Press, 1957.
An invaluable source of information and insight on Soviet communist party life, based on voluminous party records captured by the German Army during World War II.

Fischer, Ruth
STALIN AND GERMAN COMMUNISM, Harvard University Press, 1948.

Gurian, Waldemar
BOLSHEVISM: THEORY AND PRACTICE, Macmillan, 1932.
A systematic account of the historical and social conditions which gave rise to the theory of Bolshevism, and an account of the practical results of the Russian Revolution.

Hoover, J. Edgar
MASTERS OF DECEIT, Henry Holt & Co., 1958.
The head of the FBI looks at communism.

Leites, Nathan
THE OPERATIONAL CODE OF THE POLITBURO, McGraw-Hill, 1951.
The operational beliefs of the rulers of communism.

Leonhard, Wolfgang
CHILD OF THE REVOLUTION, Regnery, 1958.
An autobiography of a former leading German communist who was reared, educated and trained in the Soviet Union for his position as a professional communist functionary.

Meyer, Frank S.
THE MOULDING OF COMMUNISTS, Harcourt, Brace & Co., 1961.

A perceptive account of the training of hard-core communist party cadres.

Rossi, A.
  A COMMUNIST PARTY IN ACTION, Yale University Press, 1949.
    Written by a former official of the French Communist Party, it highlights the political and military organization of the party along with its activities among intellectuals and youth.

Schapiro, Leonard
  THE ORIGIN OF THE COMMUNIST AUTOCRACY, Harvard University Press, 1956.
    A graphic account of Lenin's creation, from 1917 to 1922, of all the characteristic institutions of Soviet totalitarian rule.

Schapiro, Leonard
  THE COMMUNIST PARTY OF THE SOVIET UNION, Random House, 1960.
    The most comprehensive, up-to-date, one-volume history available.

Serge, Victor
  THE CASE OF COMRADE TULAYEV, Doubleday, 1950.
    A novel, written in the West, about thought and life in the communist movement.

Shub, David
  LENIN, Doubleday, 1948.
    A biography.

Wolfe, Bertram D.
  THREE WHO MADE A REVOLUTION, Dial Press, 1948.
    A biography of Lenin, Trotsky and Stalin with emphasis on their role in the Communist Party.

Chapter 3

Communist Tactics

THE YEARS from 1900 to the Bolshevik Revolution in 1917 were a period of blueprinting by Lenin of the principles of strategy and of his struggles to build a party with which to gain power.

The history of communist tactics may be said to begin with the Bolshevik Revolution. In that history, up to the present time, eight principal periods may be distinguished.

What Was the First Period of Communist Tactics?

The first period opened with the Bolshevik Revolution and ended about 1921. This was the phase of the consolidation of power by the Bolshevik state and of the fostering of immediate world-wide revolution. It was responsible for the revolutionary tide which engulfed a great part of Europe after World War I.

In this phase occurred the civil war and the Allied intervention in Soviet Russia. This was the period of "war communism" in Soviet Russia, marked by the forcible requisition of grain from the peasants, the creation of labor armies under military discipline, and other extreme measures.

In this phase the Comintern was established to organize the world revolution and bolster Soviet Russia.

What Was the Second Period of Communist Tactics?

The second period, from 1921 to 1928, was basically a transition stage of communist tactics.

It began, following victory in the civil war and failure of the revolutionary upsurge in Europe to achieve success, with the adoption in Soviet Russia of a moderate economic policy. This was known as the New Economic

61

Policy, and it remained in force until adoption of the first five-year plan.

While waiting for revival of the world revolution, Lenin projected the policy of resuming relations with "capitalist states." Under the Treaty of Rapallo of 1922, Soviet Russia and Germany undertook political and military collaboration against the Versailles system. In this stage, Lenin also initiated the united front policy of collaboration with socialists in other countries.

After Lenin's illness and death, there occurred the tremendous struggle between Stalin and Trotsky over communist tactics. As Stalin controlled the party and state apparatus, communist tactics during this stage became increasingly nationalistic in substance and somewhat, but not altogether, nationalist in form.

Stalin destroyed the opposition in 1927-28, and the Sixth Congress of the Third International, in the latter year, adopted the Comintern program which embodied his concepts of communist tactics.

This marked the end of the second period and the opening of the third period of communist tactics.

What Was the Third Period of Communist Tactics?

In the period from 1928 to 1935 two goals were sought: on the one hand, the defense and development of the U.S.S.R. as the bastion of world communism; on the other hand, overt extreme revolutionism, the attainment of the world-wide collapse of capitalism, and the triumph of communism everywhere as a result of wars between the capitalist powers and destructive depressions in these countries.

During these years, industry in the U.S.S.R. was developed rapidly under the first five-year plan. Agriculture was collectivized forcibly, resulting in a man-made famine in which several million peasants perished; and the social structure of the Soviet Union was profoundly modified—a new elite ruling class of several million was created. Slave labor assumed tremendous proportions.

In the democratic countries, which were in the throes of economic depression, the Communist International pursued a general policy of revolutionary extremism. In the communist view, this was the "third period," following the first period of revolutionary upsurge and the second of capitalist stabilization. Now, the world revolution again stood as the "order of the day."

At the same time, the communists abandoned the tactic of the united front, which had more or less characterized their second period. They refused all collaboration with the socialists and other democrats, whom they denounced as "social fascists," and they split the unions and other working class organizations controlled by socialists and other democratic forces.

In Germany, the communists collaborated with the Nazis against the socialists. They offered no organized resistance to Hitler's assumption of power—on the theory that the Nazi triumph would only exacerbate Germany's political and economic ills, and power would then fall to the communists.

What Was the Fourth Period of Communist Tactics?

The communist tactics of this period—which began with the Seventh Congress of the Comintern in Moscow in August, 1935 and lasted exactly four years, until the signing of the Hitler-Stalin Pact in August, 1939—were motivated by a new-found fear of the Nazi regime. By 1935 Stalin began to realize that Hitler meant business and Moscow feared that the powerful Nazi state, which had begun to disappoint Soviet hopes for continued German-Soviet collaboration, would become the spearhead of a coalition of powers against the U.S.S.R. And indeed, by 1936, Hitler had already constructed his Anti-Comintern Pact, with Mussolini's Italy and Tojo's Japan as his partners.

Reflections of this fear were to be seen in the sweeping purges of 1935-39 in the U.S.S.R. which destroyed the greater part of the generation of Bolsheviks who had made the revolution, fought in the civil war, and built the Soviet state. Among other things, the victims were accused of espionage and treachery on behalf of Nazi Germany.

Communist strategy to prevent a Nazi-led, anti-Soviet coalition centered on the collective security policy of the Soviet government and a revived popular front policy of the Comintern.

The popular front policy called for a coalition of communist, socialist, democratic and progressive forces against fascist and reactionary elements. In a number of instances it was conspicuously successful in building communist strength.

The real objective of the collective security policy was to sharpen existing differences among the European powers. The Soviet Union joined the League of Nations, denounced by Lenin as an imperialist "thieves' kitchen." It made alliances with France and Czechoslovakia, directed against Germany. In 1935, it denounced the Italian conquest of Ethiopia, which threatened British domination of east Africa and the Red Sea, but it supplied the Italian navy with oil. In the Spanish civil war of 1936-39, the Soviet government intervened on the side of the republican government against the fascists supported by Germany and Italy.

In 1939, the Soviet government, alarmed by Hitler's triumph at Munich in 1938 in dismembering Czechoslovakia, undertook simultaneous negotiations with England for an alliance against Germany, and with Germany for an alliance directed against France and England. The outcome was the infamous Nazi-Soviet pact.

What Was the Fifth Period of Communist Tactics?

This period, from August, 1939 until June, 1941, opened with the partition of Poland in accordance with the secret clauses of the Nazi-Soviet pact. During the war when Germany fought England and France, the Soviet Union supplied Germany with wheat, oil, and other essential materials.

The communists denounced the war as an imperialist struggle. Stalin, writing in *Pravda,* official organ of the Soviet Communist Party, charged England and France with responsibility for the war. Vyacheslav Molotov, Soviet Minister of Foreign Affairs, declared that "Hitlerism . . . is a matter of taste." *Izvestia,* official organ of the Soviet government, supported Hitler's proposals of October 8, 1939, for ending the war, including settlement of the "Jewish problem." In France, the communists spoke of turning the imperialist war into civil war. In the United States, the communists opposed the draft, lend-lease, and other measures, and sponsored the slogan, "The Yanks Are Not Coming."

The communist strategy employed in Europe to buttress the U.S.S.R. and to pit the powers against one another, was applied also in Asia. In 1938, Japan and the Soviet Union had fought a short but full-scale undeclared war along the Soviet-Manchurian border. In April, 1941, when Japanese preparations for war with the United States were well advanced, the Soviet government signed a five-year neutrality pact with Japan, which included Soviet recognition of the Japanese puppet state in Manchuria. The Soviet government thus secured its position in the Far East, at the expense of China and the United States, and sold out the Chinese communists who were waging guerilla war against the Japanese in Manchuria.

In Asia, Soviet strategy was momentarily successful. But in Europe, expanding Soviet power threatened vital German interests in eastern Europe and was a powerful factor in Hitler's decision to attack the U.S.S.R., in June, 1941.

What Was the Sixth Period of Communist Tactics?

This was the period, from June, 1941 until May, 1945, of the "Great Patriotic War" and the "National War of Liberation" against Germany and of the Soviet-American-British coalition against the fascist axis.

After Germany invaded the Soviet Union on June 22, 1941, the communist parties in the free countries reversed their attitude on the war, demanding in chorus with the Soviet government that their own governments open a second front in Europe to aid the Soviet armies. In the United States, the communists became super patriots and now shouted, "The Yanks Are Not Coming Too Late."

In 1943, the Comintern was dissolved on the ground

that it was "a hindrance to the . . . national workers' parties." In reality it was superfluous. Its dissolution was a convenient and deceitful sop to the anti-communist sentiments of the Soviet Union's allies in the wartime coalition. In the United States, the Communist Party enacted a farce in "dissolving" itself and forming the Communist Political Association. Browder, then Stalin's loyal American minion, proclaimed his acceptance of free enterprise.

But as Russian armies cleared the Soviet Union of the enemy and pursued the Nazis into their homeland, Soviet imperialism realized new and greater opportunities. At conferences with the United States and England in 1943 and 1945, the Soviet government won recognition of a "security" zone in eastern Europe and the promise of large territorial and strategic advantages as its reward for its agreement to enter what all then thought would be the long and costly war against Japan.

Altogether, by the end of the war, the Soviet world had been enlarged by part or all the territory and population of more than ten states in eastern and central Europe and Asia. In total, the Soviet world gained some 260,000 square miles and extended its sway over approximately 125,000,000 additional victims. And all this preceded the conquest of China.

What Was the Seventh Period of Communist Tactics?

This period lasted from the end of World War II until the death of Stalin in March, 1953.

The end of World War II found the Soviet Union in military occupation of a vast territory in eastern and central Europe. It proceeded to consolidate this area into an empire of satellite states with the same social system as its own. In Asia, it created a satellite in North Korea and gave enormous aid to the Chinese communists. The conquest of China by Mao Tse-tung altered the world balance of forces to the advantage of communism and opened a new epoch in the history of Asia.

The United States, supported by the West European states and countries in Asia and Latin America, challenged the expansionist drive of communist imperialism and undertook to contain it. Post-war differences developed into a cold war between the Soviet and democratic worlds. Communist strategy in the "cold war" comprised four principal sets of tactics:

1) Sustained attempts by the communist parties to weaken the economy and political life of the western countries, especially in France and Italy, and also in West Germany;

2) Armed uprisings and prolonged rebellions by guerrillas, as in Greece in 1946-49, and in French Indo-China, which in 1954 led to an uneasy truce between communist and non-communist forces;

3) Open aggression by the communist state of North Korea against the non-communist state of South Korea, with the support of the Chinese communists; and

4) Propaganda and diplomatic campaigns for peace and disarmament to divert attention from the steadily mounting Soviet war preparations; propaganda and diplomatic offensives against "American imperialism" as the aggressor in Korea against the peoples of Asia and as instigator of atomic war to destroy the Soviet world; and diplomatic maneuvers designed to sharpen differences between the United States and its allies over such issues as negotiation of peace in Korea, disposition of Formosa, and the seating of Communist China in the United Nations.

What Is the Eighth Period of Communist Tactics?

This is the period from Stalin's death to date. Actually, it has been a period characterized by a number of fluctuations in the Party line and tactics, resulting chiefly from the struggle for power in the Kremlin, the uncertainties about who would emerge as his victorious successor, and the consequent lack of assurance about the future of the leadership and policy in Moscow and throughout the whole international communist movement.

Thus, shortly after Stalin's death on March 5, 1953, while the struggle for his succession raged behind the scenes, a series of crises shook the Soviet world. With the bloody tyrant gone, workers, peasants, intellectuals and most other segments of the population began to hope that some of the worst features of his tyranny throughout the Soviet empire would be eliminated. Quite spontaneously, people undertook demonstrations for better economic conditions and a loosening of the totalitarian political reins. Presumably, many people felt that the disorder in the ranks of the communist leadership might provide an opening for such improvements.

The demonstrations began with the unprecedented uprising of workers in East Berlin on June 17, 1953, and was followed in quick order by similar strikes in other parts of East Germany, and among organized Czech factory workers, Hungarian peasants, Bulgarian tobacco workers, and even the slave laborers of Siberia. The historic uprising in East Berlin was quickly suppressed by the use of Soviet tanks and soldiers, against whom the rocks, stones and slogans of the heroic workers were obviously futile.

Even more unprecedented was the reaction of the various communist governments. Unsure of the outcome of the power struggle in Moscow and evidently getting no firm directives from there as to how to handle the uprisings, they fell back to a more defensive posture. Instead of executing all participants, as they would have done under Stalin, they compromised. The strikers remained unmolested when they returned to work, and far-reaching governmental reforms were projected and, to some extent, undertaken.

On the domestic front, a new course of action was undertaken which appreciably modified the existing repressive policies. This was especially true for the satellite countries where people still could remember living conditions under democracy. Economic concessions, such as price reductions, cancellations of tax arrears, reduced farm delivery quotas and, most significant of all, a shift from heavy to light industry, were the norms. Political relaxation included amnesties, decline in purges, relaxation of governmental direction of cultural and scientific activity, and the avowal to cooperate with the landowning peasants.

Foreign policy was equally conciliatory. The tempo of the "peace offensive" was stepped up, cultural delegations crossed the iron curtain from both sides with increasing frequency, and Malenkov spoke of the terrors of the "A-Bomb" and of the futility of war. Only the Chinese struck a discordant note, humiliating France and the free world at the Geneva conference early in 1954, by enforcing the partition of French Indo-China. In order to reassure both the Russian people and the outside world against the spectre of a new Stalin, collective leadership was incessantly stressed.

This state of affairs did not last long. As the struggle for supremacy in the Kremlin reached a crisis, the line changed again: the key to the change in the line was the shifting alliances that were made by Nikita Khrushchev in his rise to power. He followed the old Stalin-Rakosi prescription of "salami tactics" in destroying every effective opposition to his taking power.

At first, he allied himself with Malenkov, Bulganin, Molotov, Kaganovitch and Marshal Zhukov, the Soviet war hero, in destroying the chief of the secret police (MVD) Lavrenti Beria. Each of these men had reason to fear Beria's use of the MVD for his own power aspirations, and he was executed in June, 1953.

The period of domestic and international conciliatory tactics coincided with Malenkov's premiership. But then Khrushchev proceeded to ally himself with the "tough" faction in the Kremlin leadership to eliminate Malenkov. This was achieved in February, 1955, when Khrushchev's ally Bulganin became premier. The tough faction then proceeded to tighten the reins again. At home, first priority was again given to the production of armaments and heavy industry, to the neglect of consumer goods. Foreign policy, too, hardened for a time; Marshal Zhukov, the newly appointed defense minister, warned in an official speech that Russia was not afraid of America's atomic weapons.

As soon, however, as Khrushchev felt himself strong enough, he began to move against his allies in the "tough" camp, chiefly the old Stalinists, Molotov and Kagano-vitch.

This move against his "tough" allies was reflected in both domestic and foreign policy. In the former, for example, while the emphasis on heavy industry and armaments remained intense, Khrushchev began to call for a concomitant increase in consumer goods. In foreign policy, the Kremlin also became more conciliatory. It participated in a "summit meeting" of Big Four leaders at Geneva in the summer of 1955, and friendly overtures to the West became the order of the day.

What Was the Purpose of Khrushchev's Secret Speech of 1956?

By February, 1956, when the 20th Congress of the CPSU convened in Moscow—the first such meeting since 1952 and the first since Stalin's death—Khrushchev felt strong enough to undertake a major coup.

The fundamental import of the "secret report" he made to the Congress was to downgrade Stalin: he presented him as a paranoid megalomaniac, especially in the last eight years of his life and accused him of perpetrating a whole series of criminal acts—though Khrushchev's citation of these acts was significantly far from exhaustive. A tremor shook the whole communist world when it heard of this violent attack, for Stalin had for thirty years been the virtual godhead of the movement.

Khrushchev had several purposes in making this attack. In the first place, he desired to give the people, and the new privileged elite class of managers, technicians and middle stratum officials who had risen in the post-Revolutionary generation, some assurance that the sanguinary rule of terror was over. People wanted some relief from the total fear they had lived with for decades, and the destruction of the symbolism and "cult of personality" of Stalin was a dramatic means of giving assurances of relief.

Khrushchev also used this attack on Stalin to destroy the power of the old Stalinists completely—and soon

Molotov and Kaganovitch were demoted and, in effect, exiled.

By this means, too, Khrushchev sought to shake up the whole structure of the party at home and abroad in a drastic fashion—and soon old office-holders, Party and government officials began to be replaced with new appointees. Khrushchev thus systematically began to create his own power regime, supported by his own chosen functionaries. It was, in sum, a repetition of precisely the same means by which Stalin systematically achieved one-man rule over the period from 1924 to 1928.

What Was the Effect of De-Stalinization in the Satellites?

The policy of downgrading Stalin produced uncertainty and insecurity in the minds of party officials, and raised to the surface the people's hopes, aspirations and even demands for a better life. The effect was like that of lifting the cover slightly from a kettle of boiling water: a small amount of steam emerges. But if the water keeps boiling, it will sooner or later blow the lid off entirely—or else the lid has to be clamped down as tightly as before.

Thus, in June and July of 1956, workers in Poznan and other Polish cities streamed out of their factories to demonstrate under the slogan of "Bread and Freedom." Polish military and police forces suppressed the demonstrations bloodily, but Polish resentments against Soviet domination and communist exploitation were not stilled. On the contrary, four months later, in October, 1956, they precipitated what is known as the "Polish October" (in symbolic recollection of the Bolshevik Revolution, which had also taken place in October).

What Was the "Polish October"?

It was, in effect, a bloodless half-revolution to meet the exigencies of the moment: it represented a desperate, uneasy effort by the communist leadership to keep the lid slightly off the kettle so as to allow some steam to escape.

The stifled resentments of Polish workers, peasants

and intellectuals had become even more intense as a result of the suppression of the Poznan demonstration. By the middle of October, the atmosphere in Poland, especially in Warsaw, was heavy with the threat of violence and civil war. The frightened Polish communist leadership saw no alternative but to recall to power, as First Secretary of the Polish Communist Party, Wladyslaw Gomulka, who in 1951 had been demoted, disgraced and imprisoned as a "Titoist," and who had a reputation among the Poles as a communist who was slightly more independent of Moscow and more concerned for Poland's welfare than his more rigid Stalinist colleagues.

Gomulka came to power on October 20, cheered on, as the "lesser evil," by masses of people throughout the country. The same day, Khrushchev and his closest Kremlin cohorts arrived in Warsaw to the accompaniment of the movement of Soviet troops around the city. In a showdown between the two communist leaders, Gomulka warned that the Soviet use of force to preserve the old-line Stalinist regime in Poland would lead to war and civil war. Khrushchev, evidently persuaded that this was so, and that Gomulka, a steadfast and loyal communist for decades, was the only man who could save the situation for communism in Poland, and at the same time keep the country within the Soviet bloc, relented. Political and economic concessions were made by Moscow to Poland.

The key to this unprecedently triumphant defiance of Moscow by a satellite lay in Khrushchev's belief that Gomulka did not represent any sort of threat to Khrushchev's leadership in the international communist movement and to the U.S.S.R.'s unquestioned supremacy in foreign affairs. It was not, as events in Hungary just one week later were to demonstrate, any reluctance on Moscow's part to use force in the face of what it considered an unmistakable revolt for freedom from its domination.

The success of Gomulka's regime since October, 1956 has rested on one factor—the people's realization that they have no alternative. This conviction stems, in turn, from certain clear facts, such as the continued presence of large Soviet forces inside Poland as well as on the Soviet-Polish frontier, and the demonstrated inability of the Western powers to help the Polish people achieve their freedom. The regime's understanding with the Catholic Church in Poland for a minimal degree of religious liberty has also helped stabilize the situation.

For about a year after 1956, Gomulka granted various political and economic concessions to the workers, the peasantry and the intellectuals—certain foods were made more available, living conditions were slightly improved, a stop was put to farm collectivization, writers were given somewhat more freedom of expression. But toward the end of 1957, the regime began to tighten the reins again in all of these areas.

What Was the Meaning of the Hungarian Revolution?

The process of de-Stalinization had repercussions in Hungary as well as in Poland, both on the party leadership and on the people. The people became increasingly restive and the leadership grew correspondingly insecure, uncertain and frightened. As early as mid-1953, Hungarian intellectuals and writers began with increasing boldness and explicitness to discuss the need for less party control of cultural and artistic life. They, and the people at large, were encouraged when Imre Nagy, a communist leader who had been in disrepute for several years, became premier in 1953. His tenure in office, marked by a certain leniency in political and economic policies, coincided with the period of Soviet leadership headed by Malenkov. And soon after Malenkov's demotion and a turn to a tougher line in Moscow in 1955, Nagy too was ousted, and the arch-Stalinist Matyas Rakosi resumed his rigid terroristic rule.

This only served to exacerbate the resentments of growing numbers of Hungarians in all walks of life— chiefly the intellectuals, students and workers. As the people grew more restive, the regime grew more tyrannical. By mid-1956, the Rakosi regime, unsettled by the trauma of Soviet de-Stalinization, felt forced to make one small concession after another, beginning with the resignation of Rakosi. The lid was slightly off the kettle of furiously boiling water, and it was too late to put it back on tightly and impossible to keep it in suspension. On October 23, 1956, the lid blew off completely.

Inspired by the events of a few days before in Poland, groups of workers and students began to issue manifestos for liberalization of life in their country. On October 23, many of them spontaneously moved toward key symbolic positions of communist power in Budapest—a statue of Stalin and the headquarters of the hated, dreaded Hungarian secret police. Thousands congregated before them, pulled down the statue and tried to storm the headquarters as well as the offices of the official radio station. The secret police opened fire on the crowds, and thus began the short-lived revolution in which some 25,000 people were slaughtered.

Swift-moving events saw the recall of Nagy to power, less as a leader of a revolution than its slightly confused symbol; Moscow's decision, made on the spot by Deputy Premier Anastas Mikoyan, to quell the revolt; the subsequent Soviet agreement, in the face of continued and even growing Hungarian resistance, to withdraw from Budapest at the end of October; Nagy's declaration of Hungarian neutrality and withdrawal from the Warsaw Pact; and finally, the Soviet decision, made as early as November 1, to intervene forcibly a second time, a decision that was implemented by the return of massive Soviet military forces to Budapest and the wholesale crushing of the revolt. In addition to the tragic number of casualties, some 125,000 Hungarians, most of them youths and many of them Freedom Fighters, fled into Austria to escape the certain doom that awaited them at the hands of the Soviets and the reconstituted Hungarian secret police. Nagy himself was replaced by Janos Kadar, a pliable tool of Moscow; two weeks later, Nagy and his closest political friends and advisors and their families were arrested and imprisoned despite a Soviet-guaranteed safe-conduct. In

1958, Moscow and Budapest revealed that they had been tried in secret and executed. The Hungarian Revolution had gone down to defeat.

What Strategic Considerations Accounted for Moscow's Different Reactions in Poland and in Hungary?

Faced with defiance in Warsaw, the Kremlin speedily arrived at a *modus vivendi* with Gomulka. Faced with revolt in Budapest, the Kremlin responded with force.

The difference in response was accounted for by the essential difference between the Polish and the Hungarian revolts. In Gomulka, Khrushchev recognized a perfervid communist who was the only man who could control the situation inside Poland, prevent the outbreak of violent revolt, and remain a loyal supporter of Soviet strategic interests and foreign policy objectives.

In Nagy, and more importantly, in the revolution which swept him to power and actually carried him far beyond his own intentions, Khrushchev recognized an open break with Soviet hegemony, a declaration of total independence in foreign policy and of freedom in internal affairs. This was a situation which the Kremlin could not tolerate on both ideological and strategic grounds.

The clear object lesson of the Hungarian Revolution was that the Kremlin was willing to risk Western displeasure and indignation—perhaps even to risk war—for the sake of retaining its hold on the empire it has molded since 1945.

How Did the Free World Respond to the Hungarian Revolution and Its Object Lesson?

The free world's sympathies were clearly with the Freedom Fighters, and the brutal Soviet repression aroused fierce indignation—perhaps all the fiercer because it was wholly impotent.

Undoubtedly Khrushchev calculated, when he unhesitatingly took the risk of bloody intervention, not only that the West's protests at the time would not be followed through, but that it would forget the object lesson and that indignation and protest and even recollection of the Revolution would soon die down in the West. For this was precisely what happened.

Bibliography

Bailey, Geoffrey
THE CONSPIRATORS, Harper, 1960.
A factual account, which reads like international detective fiction, of intrigue between Russia and western Europe during the years before World War II.
Beloff, Max
THE FOREIGN POLICY OF SOVIET RUSSIA, Royal Institute of International Affairs, 1945.
A carefully documented study of Soviet diplomacy.
Dallin, David
SOVIET FOREIGN POLICY AFTER STALIN, Lippincott, 1961.
A long-standing authority on Soviet foreign policy evaluates the crucial developments of the past eight years.
Dennen, Leon
THE SOVIET PEACE MYTH, National Committee for a Free Europe, Inc., 1951.
The facts behind the Soviet "peace" movements.
Feis, Herbert
CHURCHILL, ROOSEVELT, STALIN, Princeton University Press, 1957.
BETWEEN WAR AND PEACE, Princeton University Press, 1960.
The first volume deals with the famous summit conference at Yalta; the second, with the Potsdam summit conference. Together, they present a fully documented account of the complexities of Big Three relations during and after World War II.

Fischer, Louis

THE SOVIETS IN WORLD AFFAIRS: 1917-1929, Princeton University Press, 1951 (second edition).

An authoritative source book for this crucial period.

Goodman, Elliot R.

SOVIET DESIGN FOR A WORLD STATE, Columbia University Press, 1960.

Communist global objectives studiously analyzed.

Kennan, George F.

RUSSIA LEAVES THE WAR, Princeton University Press, 1956.

THE DECISION TO INTERVENE, Princeton University Press, 1958.

The distinguished American diplomat and historian presents in these two volumes a scholarly chronicle of Soviet-American relations in the years, 1917-1920.

RUSSIA AND THE WEST UNDER LENIN AND STALIN, Atlantic-Little, Brown, 1961.

A survey of three decades of East-West relations by an authority.

Lasky, Melvin J. (editor)

THE HUNGARIAN REVOLUTION, Praeger, 1957.

The story of the uprising as recorded in documents, dispatches, and eye-witness accounts.

Meray, Tibor

THIRTEEN DAYS THAT SHOOK THE KREMLIN, Praeger, 1959.

An inside account by a former leading Hungarian writer who was an intimate of Imre Nagy.

Rush, Myron

THE RISE OF KHRUSHCHEV, Public Affairs Press, 1958.

A thorough analysis.

Seton-Watson, Hugh

FROM LENIN TO KHRUSHCHEV, Praeger, 1960.

A history of Russia under Soviet rule.

Sontag, Raymond S. and Beddie, James S., Ed.

NAZI-SOVIET RELATIONS, 1939-1941, Department of State, Washington, D. C., 1948.

> Documents from the Archives of the German Foreign Office.

United Nations Document A/3592

REPORT OF THE SPECIAL COMMITTEE ON HUNGARY, United Nations, 1957.

> The soberly factual UN Committee's meticulous demonstration of Soviet illegality in the Hungarian Revolution.

Chapter 4

Communist Techniques

How Does the Communist Movement Try to Weaken and Destroy the Democratic World?

THE INTERNATIONAL communist movement uses two basic tactics to achieve its ends: armed force and political warfare. These tactics, in all their variety of permutations and combinations, were originally formulated by Lenin and by the Comintern under him and Stalin, and are today perpetuated by Khrushchev, Mao Tse-tung and their colleagues in every part of the world.

The tactical guide lines laid down by Lenin, and carried through in expanded and flexible form by his successors, cover methods for the weakening of existing institutions, methods for subversion of representative government, the duties of elected communist representatives, and the use of armed force.

How Do Communists Weaken Existing Institutions?

Their main attack is on law and representative government.

For obvious reasons, communists prefer a state of affairs in which they can function legally. But because they regard the state as the "executive committee of the ruling class" with which they consider themselves perpetually at war, communists, in the words of the Statutes of Admission to the Comintern,

". . . can have no confidence in bourgeois laws . . ."

Where the law forbids communist activity, the Statutes directed, the communists must find a way of acting legally through "front" parties and organizations and, at the same time, must continue to function illegally.

". . . a combination of legal and illegal work is absolutely necessary."

How Do Communists Undermine
Representative Government?

The Second Congress of the Comintern made the answer to this question unmistakably clear in *The Communist Party and Parliamentarism.*

The guiding thought is:

". . . bourgeois parliaments . . . cannot be taken over by the proletariat . . .

"The task of the proletariat consists in blowing up . . . all the parliamentary institutions . . . whether they be republican or constitutional monarchy.

"The same applies to the local government institutions."

The "fundamental means" of accomplishing this task was defined as "mass demonstrations . . . carried out . . . under the direction of a . . . Communist Party" and "logically leading to an uprising against the capitalist state."

It is necessary "in this warfare . . . developing into civil war" to "secure every and all legal positions making them . . . auxiliaries in the revolutionary work, and subordinating such positions to the . . . mass struggle."

Chief among such "auxiliary supports" are election campaigns and "the rostrum of parliament."

Elected communist party candidates enter parliament as "scouting parties" in order to prepare "the masses to blow up the whole bourgeois machinery and parliament itself from within."

This work of "preparation of a proletarian uprising . . . for the destruction of the bourgeois state and for the creation of the new proletarian state" consists "chiefly in making revolutionary propaganda from the parliamentary platform . . ."

But "if the Communists have the majority in the local government institutions, they must:

a) carry on revolutionary propaganda against the bourgeois central authority;

b) . . . attempt to establish an armed workers' militia . . .

c) under certain conditions substitute local Workers' Councils (soviets) for the municipal administration."

What Are the Duties of Communist Representatives?

In every country, elected representatives, including communists, take an oath, prescribed by law, which generally commits the swearer to uphold the laws and government of his country.

Nevertheless, *The Party and Parliamentarism* directed:

"Each communist representative must remember that he is not a 'legislator' who is bound to seek agreements with other legislators, but an agitator of the party, detailed into the enemy's camp in order to carry out the orders of the party there.

"The communist member is answerable not to the wide mass of his constituents, but to his own communist party—whether legal or illegal."

The communist representative must propose "demonstrative measures, not for the purpose of having them passed . . . but for the purposes of propaganda, agitation, and organization . . ."

He must get "preliminary instructions" on all important political questions from the central committee of the party to which he must submit "for confirmation" the "thesis of his speech, or the text," at each "forthcoming important debate."

He "is bound to combine legal work with illegal work."

He must use his "inviolability," or parliamentary immunity from arrest, to render "assistance to the illegal organizations . . ."

The communist movement, it is clear, is always partly or entirely conspiratorial and underground.

How Do Communists Use Armed Force to Tear Down the Democratic World?

Lenin forecast the use of armed force by a communist state against non-communist nations. Before coming to power, he wrote:

"The victorious proletariat . . . having expropriated

the capitalists and organized Socialist production at home, would rise against the rest of the capitalist world, attracting the oppressed classes of other countries, raising among them revolts against the capitalists, launching, in case of necessity, armed forces against the exploiting classes and their states."

It should again be noted, of course, that the communist use of the phrase "socialist production" has no connection at all with genuine democratic socialism, or with genuine socialist modes of production such as exist in England, Scandinavia and Israel.

What Forms Has the Communist Use of Armed Force Taken?

Since the Bolshevik Revolution, communist armed force has assumed three basic forms.

—Direct, overt military aggression. Examples: the forcible seizure of the then-independent Georgian Republic and its incorporation into the U.S.S.R. in 1921; abortive communist putsches in Germany in 1921 and 1923; Soviet encouragement of an unsuccessful communist coup in Canton, China, in 1927; the Soviet occupation of eastern Poland in September, 1939 (based on the terms of the Stalin-Hitler Pact); the conquest of Finland during World War II (an aspect of the Red Army's westward sweep against the German forces); North Korea's invasion, massively supported by armaments and money from the Soviet Union and by "volunteers" from Communist China, of South Korea in 1950; the U.S.S.R.'s suppression of the Hungarian Revolution in 1956; Communist China's assault on the Tachen Islands in 1957, resulting in the Chinese Nationalist evacuation of the islands; Communist China's incessant bombardment, since 1958, of the Nationalist-held islands of Quemoy and Matsu; Communist China's sanguinary suppression of Tibetan resistance to communist domination in 1959.

—The threat of communist armed forces massed on a neighboring country's borders. Examples: the Soviet conquest of Lithuania, Latvia and Estonia in 1940; the communist coup in Czechoslovakia in 1948; the U.S.S.R.'s attempt to seize Berlin through a blockade in 1948-49 (foiled only by the firm, united resistance of Britain, France, the United States, and the people of West Berlin).

—Insurrections by politically disciplined communist guerrilla forces. Examples: the tight bands of communist armed groups in the French and Italian anti-Nazi underground resistance movements, and the Yugoslav partisans led by Marshal Tito (all of them active in World War II); the civil war undertaken by the Chinese communists in 1945, culminating in their seizure of power in 1949; civil war conducted by communist guerrillas, aided by the neighboring communist states of Bulgaria, Albania and Yugoslavia, against the legitimate government of Greece in 1946-47 (stopped only by the resistance of the majority of the Greek people with the support of Britain and of the United States under the terms of the Truman Doctrine); civil war conducted against the French in Indo-China by communist guerrillas exploiting the anti-colonial and nationalist sentiments of the native peoples, culminating in the communist domination of the northern portion of the new state of Vietnam; communist guerrilla activities since the end of the war and until today in Indonesia, Burma, Laos and Malaya.

What Is the Communist Objective in Laos?

In the last months of 1960 and in the first half of 1961, a new world crisis emerged in the tiny Southeast Asian kingdom of Laos (population—little more than 1,000,000). In the northeast provinces of that country, communist and pro-communist guerrilla forces, trained and led by officers of neighboring communist North Vietnam and massively supplied with arms by the U.S.S.R., stepped up a campaign of infiltration, sabotage and outright military assault on the legitimate government, backed by the United States. So intent was world opinion on this explosive confrontation of the forces of East and West in this obscure part of the world, that many people tended to ignore the real objective of the communist campaign.

It is not so much Laos as the Republic of South Vietnam which the communists seek to take over. There, a staunchly anti-Communist, reform government began, in 1955, to cope with the enormous difficulties that were the legacy of 90 years of French and Japanese colonial rule. This government, headed by President Ngo Dinh Diem, undertook one of the largest and most effective land reform programs in all of Asia, while stimulating modest industrial growth. South Vietnam is the strategic and economic gateway to the entire Southeast Asian peninsula; any predatory power that controls it can also hold sway over Thailand, Cambodia, Malaya, and perhaps even Burma. During World War II the Japanese used Vietnam in just that way. It was precisely because of the growing success of South Vietnam's far-sighted economic reforms, because of the example for all of Asia that was provided by this anti-communist government working effectively in behalf of its people, that North Vietnam, backed by Communist China and the U.S.S.R., began a campaign of subversive infiltration and terror in many parts of the Republic.

When the South Vietnamese army effectively sealed off its border with North Vietnam, the Communists found a new and more deadly way of conducting their guerrilla war—through neighboring Laos, which has a long, winding border with South Vietnam, a border difficult to seal or defend because much of it is covered with jungle and mountains. Thousands of specially trained communist guerrillas have been able to filter through this border and to wreak havoc among the villages and farms of South Vietnam. As more of the Laos-South Vietnam border area has come under the control of communist guerrillas in Laos, this penetration has become more massive, easier to effect and more difficult to counter. The conquest of all or much of Laos, then, is directed at the more decisive objective of South Vietnam, which, in turn, is the key to all of Southeast Asia.

What Is the Meaning of the Cuban Revolution?

The revolution led by Fidel Castro against the bloody tyranny of Fulgencio Batista did not begin as a communist movement. It was heartily supported by the mass of the Cuban people who had had enough of the dictatorship. It was a revolution carried out in the name of democratic rights and social justice, and the revolutionary army contained not only communists, but a wide range of democratic forces.

Irrespective of Castro's previous politics, it is clear that his key advisors were communists and fellow travelers, including especially the professional Latin American communist revolutionist, Ernesto "Che" Guevara. And despite certain immediate benefits for the people—such as housing, schools and hospitals—the Castro regime was very quickly transformed into an authoritarian dictatorship increasingly inclined to the tutelage of the communist party and to a close political and economic alliance with the bloc of Soviet nations, who supplied Cuba with military and economic aid and hosts of "technicians" and other specialist advisors. So the ideals and promises of democracy and of economic and social justice, in the name of which the revolution was fought and supported by the mass of the people, were betrayed.

Cuba is today a full-fledged communist satellite—the only such, in fact, that achieved this status without the presence or threat of external Soviet force. It is an armed camp which is a military, political and ideological threat to the United States and the rest of Latin America. Cuba serves as the militant base for the export of virulent anti-Americanism, communist ideology and propaganda, and the violent exploitation of the legitimate grievances and bitterness of the oppressed or deprived masses of Latin America.

What Are the Principal Techniques of Communist Political Warfare?

Communist power constantly seeks to present itself as the very opposite of an aggressive, expansionist imperialism. It has, therefore, invariably relied heavily—indeed primarily—on an almost inexhaustible arsenal of varied *political warfare* techniques to explain away the use of armed force, to cover up its real objectives, and to delude people's minds with persuasive myths about those objectives.

The keys to communist political warfare techniques are best summed up in two communist terms—the "party line" and "transmission belts."

The party line is the specific communist position on any given issue, for which massive propaganda is to be made in order to further communist aims and serve Soviet interests.

Transmission belts refer to the vast apparatus whose function is to transmit this propaganda through the creation and manipulation of a whole array of auxiliary organizations.

Among the tactics used in this apparatus are: infiltration and manipulation of trade unions and other mass organizations, espionage, the creation of "front" organizations, manipulation of international trade, and intensification of political and racial differences.

How Does Communist Propaganda Operate?

A very special role is assigned to communist propaganda. Where the more direct tactics are impracticable or feeble, propaganda prepares the way for them; where they are effective, propaganda complements them; and where they have been successful, propaganda consolidates the victory.

Communist propaganda has two facets: domestic and foreign. At home, it is, along with political, social and police pressures, the most valuable instrument for insuring the continuing loyalty of the people by massive doses of constant indoctrination aimed at denigrating the non-communist world and glorifying the communist regime.

Outside the communist empire, enormous sums are spent annually and large numbers of party functionaries are employed, especially in Asia, Africa and Latin America, in the attempt to undermine the peoples' faith in democracy and to gain adherents to the communist cause. This propaganda is directed at all segments of the population, and every grievance held by workers, peasants, youth, intellectuals, is exploited.

Though the party has a large apparatus for direct propaganda aimed at winning members or voters for itself, by far the larger and more dangerous apparatus is that which the party has created for indirect propaganda. This is the apparatus of auxiliaries—the transmission belts—of individuals, organizations, and institutions. They include fellow travelers, front groups, special campaign organizations and special schools.

What Is a Fellow Traveler?

A fellow traveler is a person who knowingly supports communist policy and collaborates with the communists in various ways, but is not a member of a communist party. He is very useful to the communists in reaching and influencing people who would be repelled by direct contact with the communist movement.

What Is a Communist Front?

A communist front is an organization ostensibly non-communist, formed to serve a liberal cause, but actually established and controlled by communists for their own revolutionary purposes. Or it is an organization which communists have captured and turned into a communist front. The activities of communist fronts are often harmful to legitimate liberal organizations which pursue democratic ideals and principles.

The Progressive Party, which ran Henry Wallace for President in the 1948 election, was, unbeknownst to many of its members, an example of the first kind of front organization. The American Labor Party in New York State, since the split in its ranks which resulted in formation of the Liberal Party in 1944, is an example of the second kind of communist front. Other communist fronts include the National Negro Congress, Civil Rights Congress, World Federation of Democratic Youth, and International Workers Order. There are scores of others listed by the Attorney General of the United States.

Though many of the communist fronts listed by the Attorney General are largely inactive today, the communist party apparatus which created and used them in the past remains vigorous and alert to any opportunities that might arise under new circumstances to create new fronts.

Since the fervent desire for peace is always strong in the hearts of free people, spurious propaganda for peace has always been one of the chief gambits used by the communist apparatus of auxiliaries and fronts. This is a danger that must be especially guarded against, in an international atmosphere where the communists are using the "peace issue" as one of their most effective weapons of political warfare.

An earlier instance of highly successful communist exploitation of this issue in the United States is presented by a front which started its existence under the name of the American League Against War and Fascism.

There are, of course, perfectly legitimate democratic groups of a genuinely pacifist nature, such as the American Friends Service Committee and other Quaker groups, the Fellowship of Reconciliation, and the War Resisters' League.

What Was the Twisted History of the American League Against War and Fascism?

In 1932, this organization was founded to spearhead communist protests against the rising menace of Germany and Italy. It refused all cooperation with non-communist groups equally interested in protesting fascism.

In 1935, in line with communism's switch to a "popular front" with other parties, the League changed its name to the American League for Peace and Democracy. It now collaborated with the same liberal forces which, only yesterday, it had called "social fascists." (During this period, the front was composed of affiliated organizations whose total membership came to nearly two million.)

In 1939, in the wake of the Stalin-Hitler pact, the

League name was changed once more, this time to the American Peace Mobilization. It now proclaimed the necessity of America's living in peace with the Nazis and fascists. Collaboration with recent liberal allies was now rejected.

In 1941, when Hitler plunged into Russia, the name of the League changed again, becoming the American People's Mobilization. Now, again, collaboration with other groups was the order of the day.

The organization had followed diligently the twists and turns of the "party line," while pretending to be politically independent and morally pure.

Another type of highly effective communist front on an international scale was that created by the Soviet Union itself under the name of the Jewish Anti-Fascist Committee.

What Was the Jewish Anti-Fascist Committee?

In October, 1939, one month after the partition of Poland in accordance with the Nazi-Soviet pact, Victor Alter and Henry K. Erlich, prominent Jewish labor leaders of Poland, were arrested and imprisoned by the Soviet government. In September, 1941, after the abrogation of the pact and the invasion of Russian territory by its former friend and partner, Russia released the two men from their Moscow prison. The Soviet government felt that Alter and Erlich would be able to help them in what was now a war for Russian survival. They were Polish, they were Jewish and they were labor leaders. Indeed, immediately after their release, Erlich and Alter issued a call to all Polish citizens to join the new Polish army, then being organized under Soviet auspices, to fight against the Nazis.

The two men also presented a plan for organizing a Jewish anti-Hitlerite committee. It aimed to "mobilize Jews throughout the world for the struggle against Hitlerism, to organize aid and assistance to the Jewish masses in countries under Nazi control" and to serve as a relief agency for Jewish refugees in the Soviet Union. The Committee would also maintain contact with the underground movement in Poland. The Alter-Erlich plan was projected along purely democratic lines, assuring representation on the Committee to Jewish delegates from Poland, Czechoslovakia, Rumania and other Nazi-dominated countries.

After having served their function in providing the Soviet government with the means of organizing and controlling anti-Nazi sentiment in the German-dominated countries, Alter and Erlich were re-arrested and shot. In a few short months, a new organization called the Jewish Anti-Fascist Committee made its appearance. Having appropriated the Alter-Erlich idea, the Soviets proceeded to pervert it to their own purposes.

The Committee no longer put its main emphasis on helping persecuted Jews, nor did it aim to help the Allies generally. It was now dedicated to enlist world support for the Soviet Union in particular. The Jewish Anti-Fascist Committee, now the direct instrument of the U.S.S.R., was used as a propaganda machine for generating world support for the efforts of the Red Army and to spread throughout the world the story of Soviet "accomplishments." This became its exclusive function.

By 1948, with the end of the war and the emergence of the real nature of Soviet aims, plus the stepping-up of the anti-Jewish campaign, the Committee had ceased to be an effective instrument for U.S.S.R. propaganda abroad. It was therefore suppressed.

What Are Some of the Effective Communist Fronts in France Today?

Every country in the world, including even those where the party apparatus as such is small, has an effective apparatus of auxiliaries, crypto-communist organizations and fronts functioning today.

In France alone, where the party is especially strong, 140 such groups exist, each with its own offices, staff and publications. Their objectives are sometimes apparent from their names and at other times disguised. Among them are the following:

The General Confederation of Workers, Fighters for Peace, France-U.S.S.R., the International Association of Democratic Lawyers, the French University Union, the Association for Municipal Studies and Information, the Sport and Gymnastic Federation of Labor, the Committee for the Development of International Trade, the Association of Scientific Workers, the National Union of Intellectuals, the Friends of Nature, the Federation of Rent-Payers, the People's Musical Federation.

What Are Some Effective Communist Fronts in Asia and Africa Today?

Communist front organizations seek to play an important and decisive role in underdeveloped, ex-colonial countries. Since proto-Soviet propaganda there chiefly exploits nationalistic and anti-colonial feelings, the true face of communism is almost completely hidden. Random examples of some of these groups are:

The Association for the Advancement of Asian Peoples, the Union of the People of Cameroon, the Association of Frenchmen of Tunisia, the Study and Action Committee for Peace in Algeria, the General Union of Algerian Workers. This last has its chief headquarters in Prague.

What Are Communist Propaganda Schools?

One of the most distinctive traits of this apparatus is to establish special schools to train propagandists. France has six such schools. Moscow and Leningrad Universities have special institutes for this purpose, where such distinguished personalities as the Number Two Chinese communist, Liu Shao-chi, and President Ho Chi Minh of the Communist Vietminh Republic (North Vietnam), studied. The Arab communist leader, Khalil Bakdash, also studied there.

In 1960, following the murder of Patrice Lumumba, the pro-communist leader of the former Belgian Congo, the Soviet authorities renamed a new special college for African students the Patrice Lumumba Friendship of the Peoples University. The function of this segregated school is to prepare African students to return to their countries with some skills and friendly, complaisant attitudes toward Soviet purposes in their continent.

In Tashkent, the capital of Soviet Turkmenistan, there is a "University for Afro-Asian Studies," attended by thousands of students, chiefly from Ghana, Guinea, Sudan and Cameroon.

Prague has two schools for elites, which have been attended by such men as President Sekou Touré of Guinea, the brother of President Kwame Nkrumah of Ghana, and Raul Castro, the brother of Cuba's Premier, Fidel Castro.

In the Buriat-Mongolian Republic, Moscow has established a "seminary" to train Buddhist lamas who then spread out all over Asia, especially Tibet. Since they are of the same race as the Tibetans, they are likely to be more welcome there than the lamas trained in Peking.

But Peking has itself become the center of general schools for producing "anti-colonialist" fellow-traveling propagandists who operate throughout South and Southeast Asia.

How Do Communists Exploit Differences and Unrest?

The classic example of the exploitation of differences within a nation is, of course, Russia. When the Czarist regime was overthrown in 1917 and was replaced by a provisional democratic government, the Bolsheviks, a minority party which had played a distinctly minor role in the revolution, began its subversive agitation. By hammering on the theme—Land, Peace, Bread—during a critical period, they skillfully increased disaffection among peasants and workers, and by raising the slogan—All Power to the Soviets—they turned large numbers against the provisional government. In nine months they paved the way for the success of the armed uprising by which they came to power.

After securing power, the Bolsheviks permitted elections to a constituent assembly which they, in common with other anti-Czarist parties, had previously demanded. When the constituent assembly, in which the Bolsheviks were a minority, refused to do the bidding of the Bolshevik government, the latter dissolved it by armed force.

For Russia, which in the spring of 1917 was in the midst of a world war and in the throes of revolution, the Leninist tactics of subversion by agitation and armed insurrection were sufficient to guarantee success. For other situations in other countries, the communists subsequently developed appropriate tactics. Their greatest success was, of course, China, which will be treated in a separate section. (See Part Two, Chapter 4.)

What Is the Communist Record on the Negro Question in the United States?

Ever since its foundation in 1919-20, the Communist Party in the United States has posed as a militant champion of the Negro. Except for a small number, almost all of whom subsequently regretted their mistake, Negroes in the United States have shunned the Communist Party.

At various times and in the name of various policies, the communists have tried to exploit the grievances of the Negroes in order to promote sharp political conflict leading to civil war.

From about 1921 to 1928 they concentrated their activities on Negro industrial workers, whom they regarded as destined leaders of colonial revolutionary movements. In effect, they ignored the bulk of the Negro population, who were sharecroppers and tenant farmers in the South, and bitterly attacked the Negro middle class and the handful of Negro capitalists.

After receiving a directive from the Comintern, the American communists agitated for the next seven years, until 1935, for self-determination, including the right of secession, for Negroes in the Black Belt in the South. In this period, all Negroes were their brothers.

In 1935 the communists reversed themselves and beat the drums for a united front to realize equal rights for Negroes, that is, to win first-class citizenship for them in our society. This policy endured until 1939.

While the U.S.S.R. and Germany were allies in World War II, from 1939 to 1941, the American communists strove to use the tactic of equal rights and the slogan of self-determination, which they revived as means of opposing the Roosevelt Administration's policy of aiding England against Germany.

Then, after the Soviet Union was invaded by Germany in 1941, the communists called for "unequivocal support by Negroes of the war of National Liberation—for the 'socialist fatherland'!"

Following the onset of the Cold War, the American communists urged Negroes to "Stop Wall Street Imperialism!"

It goes without saying, of course, that Negroes in the United States have long had legitimate grievances, and are now in the process, with the aid of all Americans of democratic instincts, of pressing for the realization of their legitimate political, legal, and socio-economic aspirations. But they are moving toward this objective through bona fide democratic organizations like the National Association for the Advancement of Colored People, the National Urban League and the Congress on Racial Equality.

How Have the Communists Exploited Trade Relations?

The Soviet Union uses trade as a weapon in political controversies, as in the case of the reduction of Soviet purchases ordered from Great Britain in the 1920s and 1930s, during political disputes with that country. At times, too, it has conducted business with foreign countries in such a way as to aid local communist parties there. For example, in the spring of 1946, just before the French parliamentary elections, the U.S.S.R. offered to sell 500,000 tons of grain to France, negotiating directly with Maurice Thorez, head of the French Communist Party.

In more recent years, the Soviet Union has sought a double objective in its political use of trade and aid: steady infiltration and subversion of underdeveloped countries, and, in consequence, the ultimate cutting off of the free world's reserves of vital raw materials of which these countries possess nearly one-half. Even when it has no use for the products of an underdeveloped country, it will frequently buy up those products, if only to gain a foothold there. This is the essential meaning of the deal made in 1960 by which the Soviet Union purchased a sizable portion of Cuba's sugar production for the following three years.

In other parts of Latin America, the Soviet Union has discouraged the production of raw materials by dumping on the world market its own competitive supplies of those materials at ruinous prices. Among such raw materials are antimony, manganese and tungsten.

Both the U.S.S.R. and Communist China are now sending large numbers of technicians and supplies to various underdeveloped countries in Africa and Asia. To this they have added strategically calculated purchases of economic surpluses, such as cotton from Egypt and rice from Burma, neither of which they need. Another example of such a strategic calculation by which the communist powers and their satellites entrench themselves economically—and ultimately, politically and militarily—in underdeveloped countries is the Soviet subsidization of Egypt's construction of the vast Aswan Dam.

What Is Communist Policy on Trade Unions?

The thesis of the Second Comintern Congress on the trade union question reads in part, "Communists should have communist factions in all trade unions and factory committees, and acquire by their means an influence over the labor movement and direct it."

The aim of these factions is to "subordinate the unions to the leadership of the party . . ." in order to make of them efficient and conscious organs of the struggle for the abolition of capitalism and for the establishment of communism.

But this is not always possible. In some unions, communists are not allowed and, when discovered, are expelled. They may even be "insulted, hounded and persecuted," wrote Lenin in his *"Left Wing" Communism: An Infantile Disorder* shortly before the Second Congress.

In that case, said he,

"It is necessary to be able to withstand all this . . . if need be—to resort to all sorts of devices, maneuvers, and illegal methods, to evasion and subterfuge, in order to penetrate into the trade unions, to remain in them, and to carry on communist work in them at all costs."

On the other hand, there are situations when, from the communist point of view, it is better to split the unions.

"Placing the object and essence of labor organization higher than the form of organization," reads the thesis of the Second Congress, "the communists ought not to hesitate before a split . . . if a refusal to split would mean abandoning revolutionary work in the trade unions, and giving up the attempt to make of them an instrument of revolutionary struggle . . ."

What Is the Communist Record in Labor Unions?

In consequence of the communist attitude toward unions, the history of communist trade-union policy has rung every change from boring-from-within unions in order to capture them, to splits.

When successful in capturing unions, communists use them either to aggravate labor strife or to restrain labor from acting to improve its position, according to the needs of the moment of Soviet foreign policy.

Splits because of communist leadership of unions have resulted in a whole series of separate labor movements beginning with the Red International of Labor Unions (1921-35) and extending to the present World Federation of Trade Unions, whose claimed membership of more than fifty million includes almost thirty million in the U.S.S.R. and millions more in the Soviet satellite states.

In the view of the International Confederation of Free Trade Unions, which includes the British Trades Union Congress, the AFL-CIO, and other large affiliates, the WFTU is not a true trade-union movement, but a tool of the Soviet government.

In the United States, the communists, disguised as liberals, began boring from within the AFL. In addition, in 1929, they established the Trade Union Unity League as their federation of revolutionary unions. Under this policy, communists worked in the AFL in order to "win over," that is, split off, "the advanced workers" and "unite" them in the T.U.U.L.

This policy, a dismal failure, was abandoned in 1935 and communists reoriented themselves away from the AFL in time to become a factor in the organizing campaigns of the CIO, following the latter's break with the AFL. They secured control of, or heavily infiltrated, unions of maritime, longshore, electrical, mine, transport, fur, warehouse, retail, office, and other workers.

During the period of communist opposition to American preparedness in World War II, following arrangement of the Nazi-Soviet pact, communist control of unions was used to promote strikes. After the Soviet Union was invaded by Hitler, the communists stifled every show of discontent by the workers in the unions under their control.

In the late 1940s, after the communists were again pursuing a course of disruption, their hold on the CIO was broken in a series of sharp struggles. Communist-controlled unions were expelled from the CIO.

Today, the united AFL-CIO maintains a vigilant guard against any communist attempts at infiltration. And on the international scene, the organization, alone and through the ICFTU, plays an important role in advancing liberal, labor and general democratic objectives while combatting communist-dominated unions in the advanced countries and communist efforts to gain control of labor movements in underdeveloped countries.

How Do Communists Conduct Espionage?

Espionage is a skilled trade, requiring specialized aptitude and personnel. Soviet espionage is conducted on a global scale by Soviet military intelligence and the MVD (the secret police). As disclosures of Soviet espionage in Canada and Australia a few years ago revealed, they function in cooperation with the Soviet diplomatic corps.

In the world-wide communist espionage net, the communist parties serve principally as recruiting services for agents. Also, by penetrating government services and winning members for the party in important industries and among research scientists they acquire a vast amount of important information and establish opportunities for the operations of spies.

Revelations of the activities of Soviet espionage rings in Canada, England, Australia, and the United States, indicate that Soviet espionage is an enormously successful enterprise.

Spies in the United States, many recruited from the ranks of the Communist Party, succeeded in the last twenty years in stealing hundreds of important military, industrial, and political secrets.

Among the military secrets are details relating to the production of the H-bomb and the plans of the atom bomb. Also the plans of sonar anti-sub devices, aircraft anti-sub radar, the proximity fuse, guided missiles, and various explosives.

The industrial secrets included precious chemical formulae, photographic and synthetic-rubber processes, and research data.

Among the political data acquired by Soviet espionage agents were the espionage files of the Justice Department and many secret dispatches from U. S. diplomatic officials.

What Is the Communist World Peace Movement?

Typical of all communist fronts is the World Peace Movement, an international communist-controlled organization which circulated the Stockholm Appeal. This was a petition to outlaw the atomic bomb and it was signed by hundreds of millions of persons in many countries, including the United States. The Appeal, described by the Cominform as the "pivot of the entire activity of the communist parties," was circulated while the North Korean aggression against South Korea was in preparation.

The real purpose of the Appeal was made clear in a speech by Mikhail Suslov, Stalin's private secretary, at a secret Cominform meeting on July 21, 1951, in Berlin. Public disclosure of the speech was made by the National

Committee For A Free Europe, in a pamphlet, *The Soviet Peace Myth* by Leon Dennen.

Suslov said that "an intensification of the campaign to condemn the atom bomb and Anglo-American imperialism would also result in the election of municipal and county councils" which under "conditions of war," if "properly politicized by party factions," would form "the basis for the formation of local Soviets."

He thought that "the great peace movement created by the Stockholm Appeal can also be used . . . to penetrate . . . unions . . . organizations of war veterans, war victims, peasant and workers' societies . . ."

But the "most significant aspect of our campaign for the Stockholm Appeal" is the success in "attracting young men who . . . are joining our military sections" and "are our assurance of successful revolutionary and insurrectionary action."

Suslov remains one of the most powerful and influential figures in the Kremlin, as a key member of the CPSU's Central Committee whose First Secretary is Nikita S. Khrushchev. The latter's views on peace and peaceful coexistence has already been clarified. (See Part One, Chapter 1, page 19.)

There are, of course, legitimate non-communist groups devoted to promoting peace, e.g., American Friends Service Committee.

What Is the Soviet Record in the United Nations?

The Soviet Union has sabotaged the work of the United Nations from the very beginning. Its chief weapon has been the veto, which, by June, 1961, was cast 82 times.

The Soviet delegates have several times walked out of the Security Council. They have refused to participate in the work of numerous U.N. agencies, such as the International Monetary Fund, the International Labor Organization and many others. Instead, they have used the United Nations as a sounding board for their propaganda, abusing the prestige of the world organization for their own purposes.

By attacking the United States, England and France as

imperialist powers and by sponsoring Communist China for a seat in the Security Council, they have attempted to create the impression that they are the protectors of the weak nations of Asia. However, the discrepancy between communist propaganda in the U.N. and communist aggressions in Korea, Tibet and Indo-China has made the free countries of Asia more aware of the dangers of communism than ever before.

In sharp contrast with the illusory promises of the communist party are the genuine advances made by the truly democratic governments of the world. It is these democratic governments which are solely responsible for the social progress which has bettered the lot of the average man. And the United States in particular, within the constitutional framework of its American democracy, has achieved significant social advances along with the highest standard of living in the world.

Bibliography

Barghoorn, Frederick C.
> THE SOVIET CULTURAL OFFENSIVE, Princeton University Press, 1960.
>> A global picture of how the Kremlin campaigns to capture men's minds.

Chambers, Whittaker
> WITNESS, Random House, 1950.
>> The political autobiography of an important former Soviet agent in the U. S.

Decter, Moshe and Rorty, James
> McCARTHY AND THE COMMUNISTS, Beacon, 1954.
>> An analysis of the late Senator Joseph McCarthy's techniques and objectives in relation to Communism in America.

Dinerstein, H. S.
WAR AND THE SOVIET UNION, Praeger, 1959.
An up-to-date study of Soviet military doctrine for the nuclear age.
Division of Research for U.S.S.R. and Eastern Europe, Office of Intelligence Research, Department of State.
SOVIET WORLD OUTLOOK, Coordinator of Psychological Intelligence, U. S. Information Agency, April, 1954.
A handbook of communist statements.
Draper, Theodore
THE ROOTS OF AMERICAN COMMUNISM, Viking, 1957.
AMERICAN COMMUNISM AND SOVIET RUSSIA, Viking, 1960.
These two volumes together present a definitive historical analysis of the formative first decade, 1919-29, of the Communist Party of the U. S.
CASTRO'S CUBA: A REVOLUTION BETRAYED, The New Leader magazine, March 27, 1961.
CUBA AND U. S. POLICY, The New Leader magazine, June 5, 1961.
These two pamphlets comprise a brief, but thorough and sober examination of the Cuban revolution.
Einaudi, Mario
COMMUNISM IN WESTERN EUROPE, Cornell University Press, 1953.
Describes the tactics of parliamentary communist parties in Italy and France.
Garthoff, Raymond C.
SOVIET MILITARY DOCTRINE, Free Press, 1952.
An exhaustive study of the interrelation between Soviet military and political doctrine.
Gouzenko, Igor
THE IRON CURTAIN, E. P. Dutton, 1948.
Revelations about the Soviet espionage ring in Canada, the United States and Great Britain by a former member of the Soviet Embassy in Canada.

Hicks, Granville
WHERE WE CAME OUT, Viking, 1954.
> A personal evaluation of the communist impact on America by a literary critic who was once a member of the party.

Hook, Sidney
HERESY YES, CONSPIRACY NO, John Day, 1953.
> A thinking liberal's guide to civil liberty and communism.

Iverson, Robert W.
THE COMMUNISTS AND THE SCHOOLS, Harcourt, Brace & Co., 1959.
> How the Communists tried to penetrate the American educational system.

Kempton, Murray
PART OF OUR TIME, Simon and Schuster, 1955.
> Historical and biographical portraits of some aspects of Communist influence in the U. S.

Lasswell, H. D.
WORLD REVOLUTIONARY PROPAGANDA, A. Knopf, 1939.
> On the nature of communist propaganda.

Lyons, Eugene
THE RED DECADE, Bobbs Merrill, 1941.
> A journalistic survey of the world of communist fronts in the U. S. in the 1930s.

Record, Wilson
THE NEGROES AND THE COMMUNIST PARTY, University of North Carolina, 1950.
> The Kremlin's attempt to exploit minority grievances described in scrupulous detail.

Roy, Ralph Lord
COMMUNISM AND THE CHURCHES, Harcourt, Brace & Co., 1960.
> A detailed study of the Communist effort to infiltrate American church organizations.

Selznick, Philip
THE ORGANIZATIONAL WEAPON, Free Press, 1959.

A study of Bolshevik strategy and tactics.

Shannon, David A.
THE DECLINE OF AMERICAN COMMUNISM, Harcourt, Brace & Co., 1959.

A history of the period, 1945-59.

Stouffer, Samuel A.
COMMUNISM, CONFORMITY AND CIVIL LIBERTIES, Doubleday & Co., Inc., 1955.

A survey and study of the reactions of Americans to communism and to those who in opposing communism would sacrifice some of the liberties which the enemy would destroy.

PART TWO

COMMUNIST RULE

Chapter 1

The Soviet Empire

How Is the Soviet World Organized?

POLITICALLY, THE Soviet world is organized, according to the communist version, as a free association of independent republics in which two types of states are distinguished: socialist states and people's republics or people's democracies.

The U.S.S.R., by its own definition, is the only socialist state. All the other nations in the Soviet world are people's democracies. A people's democracy is defined as a proletarian dictatorship without soviets, that is, as a Soviet state at a lower level of political and economic development than the U.S.S.R.

Actually, the Soviet world is in greater part an empire ruled by the government of the Soviet Union.

The U.S.S.R. is the geographic, economic, political, and military heartland of the Soviet world.

The "people's democracies" of Albania, Bulgaria, Rumania, Hungary, Poland, Czechoslovakia, the Soviet zone of Germany, and the Mongolian and Korean People's Republics as well as the Vietminh (formerly French Indo-China) in Asia are vassal states, satellites of the Soviet Union.

By its social system, Yugoslavia is akin to the Soviet world, but politically it claims it is "neutralist."

Current opinion is divided with respect to China. In one view, China, because of its vast territory, population, and resources, and its relationship to the other nations of Asia, is the most valuable of the Soviet satellites. In another view, based on the same considerations, China is a potential center of great power with its own satellites, equal in status to the U.S.S.R. and in many respects antagonistic to the latter's interests.

How Was the Soviet Empire Established?

Chiefly by force and chicanery. This was the pattern:

With the help of the victorious army of the U.S.S.R., coalition governments were established in the satellite countries. Though the communists were a minority, they held the ministries controlling the police, the armed forces, and government propaganda; they penetrated rival parties and took over unions and other mass organizations. The authentic leaders of other parties were ousted or compelled to resign and the coalitions were dominated by the communists.

Non-communist parties were still tolerated on paper at this stage, but communist-controlled unions refused to print their publications and gangs broke up their meetings while the communist-controlled police looked on.

Finally, all opposition was crushed. Other parties were dissolved or absorbed by merger with the communist party; a monolithic regime was established and the fake "new democracy" was born.

The experience of Hungary is instructive. In the elections held in 1945, the communists, who had the active support of the Soviet occupation authorities and secret police, and who were led by men trained in Moscow, received only 17% of the vote. In the succeeding years, opposition parties were outlawed and the social democrats were forced to merge with the communists. In the 1949 elections, in order to insure a parliament properly subservient to the U.S.S.R., voters were offered only a single list of candidates, featuring the names of communists and communist puppets.

How Is the Soviet Empire Controlled?

Four principal instruments are used by the U.S.S.R. in controlling its satellites. The most powerful, though least active, is the Soviet army.

The most active and important are the satellite communist parties, led by men trained in and loyal to Moscow.

A third instrument is the Soviet diplomatic corps, a direct link between the Kremlin and its outpost governments. This instrument would also include the semi-diplomatic, military and economic officials of the Warsaw Pact and the Council on Mutual Assistance.

Last, but very far from least, is the secret police of the U.S.S.R., which penetrates the satellite parties and governments, and keeps the diplomatic corps and the U.S.S.R.'s military commanders under surveillance.

What Is the Pattern of Soviet Economic Relations with the Satellites?

Under Stalin, the Soviet Union exploited its satellites, which, except for Czechoslovakia, are less developed economically, in order to build its own economy at their expense. The principal method used was the integration of the satellites' economy with that of the U.S.S.R., in such a way as to insure the satellites' dependence on the Soviet Union.

The principal means used were:

1) Trade treaties, providing for the export of armaments to the satellites, and for exchange of goods at prices favoring the U.S.S.R.;

2) Bi-national corporations, controlled by the U.S.S.R., in the major industries of the satellites;

3) Loans to the satellites, control of banks issuing notes, and dependence of the satellite currencies on the ruble;

4) Appointment by the government in Moscow of managers, directors, advisors, and experts to key industries in the satellite countries; and

5) Control of those agencies in the satellite governments which supervise the political reliability and efficiency of workers, clerks, managers, directors—in fact, of everyone.

After Stalin's death, and especially as a result of the impact of the "Polish October" and the Hungarian Revolution, these exploitative measures were substantially eliminated or weakened. And Khrushchev has introduced a far greater degree of rationality into Soviet-satellite economic relations, with the objective—largely successful— of tremendously building up the industrial-military might of the bloc as a whole. Moscow's control, thus, is no weaker than it ever was; it still controls the trade of the satellites with the non-communist world and is still the main buyer, seller, broker and clearing house for the entire Soviet empire. But this control, exercised through such institutions as the Council on Mutual Assistance, has simply been put on a more effective footing for the economic warfare which Khrushchev has explicitly declared on the non-communist world.

What Is Soviet Russification?

Soviet Russification is the policy by which the government of the U.S.S.R. dominates the ideological and cultural life of the satellites.

The program of Russification includes compulsory schooling for all communists in the history and ideology of the Bolshevik party, the "liberating role" of the army of the U.S.S.R., and the necessity and advantages of alliance with the Soviet Union.

It includes such measures as the organization of intellectuals into Soviet Friendship Societies to study and popularize the "achievements of Soviet science and technique."

Under the Russification program, the study of Russian as a second language is compulsory in all schools.

And films, plays, books, and musical works produced in the U.S.S.R. predominate in the satellite countries, yielding huge profits to producing and publishing establishments in the Soviet Union.

What Is the Iron Curtain?

The Iron Curtain, an expression popularized by Winston Churchill in a speech given in 1946, comprises the system of controls by which the government of the U.S.S.R. isolates the population of the Soviet world from the non-communist world.

This consists of the prohibition of free communication and transit, generally across national borders which are everywhere patrolled by armed guards. Under this policy diplomats are restricted in number and in their movements. Few journalists from the free world are admitted and their dispatches are censored. The culture of the western world is decried as "bourgeois cosmopolitanism."

Since Stalin's death, the Iron Curtain has been lifted to a certain extent. Suspicion, rather than hatred, of foreigners is now cultivated. The staged spy trials involving diplomats, churchmen, businessmen and newspapermen from outside the Soviet world are no longer prevalent in the U.S.S.R., though they are as common a feature of political life in China as they were under Stalin.

Under Khrushchev, cultural and technical exchanges with the non-communist world are no longer forbidden, though they still do not come anywhere near the kind of free travel and exchange characteristic of the free world. Every Soviet delegation that visits a non-communist country is prudently composed of politically reliable people, including at least one member of the secret police, and hostages, e.g., relatives, are kept at home to insure their return.

The Iron Curtain remains primarily to keep Soviet and satellite citizens from having too close a relation with the non-communist world and to keep them safely at home. Despite such precautions as barbed-wire frontiers, electrified and mined borders, and three-mile "security zones" patrolled by armed guards, millions of East Europeans have managed to escape to freedom since the end of World War II.

For example, after the end of the war, more than a million men and women, forcibly taken by the Nazis from the U.S.S.R. for slave labor and as prisoners, refused to return to the Soviet Union. They chose to remain in the free world at some personal risk.

Numerous diplomatic officials and secret police agents of the Soviet world have deserted to the haven of the free world.

A vast number of people "voted with their feet" and testified to the tyranny behind the Iron Curtain by escaping to the West. Here are some figures of the number of escapees, by country, as of 1960:

a. East Germany—3,000,000 to an estimated 3,400,-
000
b. Hungary—370,000
c. Baltic countries (Lithuania, Latvia, Estonia) —
250,000
d. Poland—210,000
e. Czechoslovakia—61,000
f. Rumania—30,000
g. Bulgaria—9,000
h. Albania—8,000

What Is Titoism?

Basically, Titoism, a form of communism, is a protest
by a small, economically underdeveloped country against
economic and political oppression by the U.S.S.R. It is
affirmation of communist nationalism against the imperialism within the Soviet world.

Tito successfully opposed Stalin's attempt to dictate
Yugoslav policy and determine the rate of industrialization and collectivization in Yugoslavia. He was successful
largely because the Yugoslav partisans had taken power
with American and British aid and because the armed
forces of the U.S.S.R. were not stationed on Yugoslav
soil.

Since Stalin's death, an uneasy *modus vivendi* has been
reached between Tito's Yugoslavia and the Soviet world.

Tito and his colleagues continue to guard the independence of their government and party as jealously as
ever. But for all that and for all the subtle modifications
of the police state regime (comparable to those instituted
by Khrushchev inside the U.S.S.R.), Yugoslavia remains
a one-party state, ruled by a hierarchy of dedicated Leninists who are committed to the ultimate establishment of
communism in their country. Civil liberties are unknown,
collectivization of agriculture and industry continues
apace, as does rigid state control over the tiny segment of
petty commercial enterprise which is allowed to small
businessmen, professionals, and some artisans.

A profound symbolic indication of the state of affairs in
Yugoslavia is the nine-year prison term, beginning in

1957, to which the former Number Two Yugoslav communist, Milovan Djilas, has been subjected. Djilas' crime was to write a series of articles exposing the intrigue and high living of the ruling party hierarchy, and subsequently a searching theoretical analysis of the inevitably dictatorial and oppressive nature of the ruling clique in any communist society. This analysis he incorporated in a book entitled *The New Class*.

But despite Yugoslavia's political independence of Moscow, Tito and his colleagues not only remain Leninists in their domestic aims, but continue, for all their "revisionist" views, to look upon the Soviet Union as a "socialist" state, which, for any Leninist, is obviously superior to non-socialist, capitalist states. This explains, for example, the fact that in international affairs, Yugoslavia has hardly veered from the line laid down in Moscow: at the United Nations, for instance, Yugoslavia has voted with the Soviet bloc on virtually every issue. Thus, the basis of the Titoist reconciliation with the Kremlin has been ideological—the undeviating acceptance of the U.S.S.R. as a socialist, Leninist state.

This has been made all the easier for Belgrade in view of Khrushchev's pragmatic acceptance of Tito's divergences. Ideologically, Khrushchev has explicitly not accepted the legitimacy of "Tito's way" to socialism. But it is worth Moscow's while to accept the status quo vis-à-vis Belgrade. For Moscow's accommodation to a "revisionist," neutralist Yugoslavia enables it to use Titoism as a cutting edge for its objectives among its satellites, in the free world, and in the neutralist world of Asia and Africa.

Among the satellites, especially among those elements who hope ultimately for a modicum of independence from Moscow's total control, this accommodation seems to hold out the hope that through the right kind of "cooperation" with Moscow, that modicum may be achieved. It thus serves to weaken those forces among the satellites who seek or hope for more complete independence of Moscow.

In the free world, this accommodation has the impact of impressing wishful thinkers with the idea that Moscow has perhaps given up its aims of world domination and is prepared for genuine peaceful coexistence.

And in the neutralist world, it has the impact of impressing some Asian and African governments and leaders with the idea that they can in the long run remain neutral and avoid being swallowed up by Soviet imperialism. This, in turn, also has a weakening effect on the free world, for it makes it all the more difficult to demonstrate to the newly independent nations of Asia and Africa that their convictions about their long-range relations with the Soviet empire are illusory.

Bibliography

Armstrong, Hamilton Fish
   TITO AND GOLIATH, Macmillan, 1951.
      Titoism and its relation to world communism.
Bolloten, Burnett
   THE GRAND CAMOUFLAGE, Praeger, 1961.
      How the Spanish Communist Party, with decisive Soviet aid, was transformed, within less than a year after the outbreak of the Spanish Civil War, from an insignificant group into the dominant force of Loyalist Spain.
Dallin, David
   THE NEW SOVIET EMPIRE, Yale University Press, 1951.
      The Soviet expansion in Europe and Asia.
Djilas, Milovan
   THE NEW CLASS, Praeger, 1957.
      A profound analysis of communism by the imprisoned former Yugoslav leader, who is one of the most important theoreticians and functionaries ever to have defected from the movement.
Kertesz, Stephen D. (ed.)
   THE FATE OF EAST CENTRAL EUROPE, University of Notre Dame Press, 1956.

A country-by-country account of the process by which the Soviet Union, in cooperation with local communist parties, took over the nations of Eastern Europe and the Baltic.

Laqueur, Walter Z.
COMMUNISM AND NATIONALISM IN THE MIDDLE EAST, Praeger, 1957.

An analysis by a leading authority on these interrelated subjects.

Martin, David
ALLY BETRAYED, Prentice-Hall, 1946.

The revealing story of how British-American wartime diplomacy lost Yugoslavia for the West in the postwar period.

Schmidt, Dana Adams
ANATOMY OF A SATELLITE, Little, Brown and Co., 1952.

The celebrated correspondent of *The New York Times* gives a first hand report of the communist coup d'état in Czechoslovakia.

Seton-Watson, Hugh
THE EAST EUROPEAN REVOLUTION, Praeger, 1951.

How the Soviet Union took over the East European countries after World War II and how it maintains its power there.

Ulam, Adam B.
TITOISM AND THE COMINFORM, Harvard University Press, 1952.

An objective presentation of the conflict between Tito and the Cominform.

U. S. Office of the High Commissioner for Germany
SOVIETIZATION OF THE PUBLIC SCHOOL SYSTEM IN EASTERN GERMANY, 1951.

How the communists sovietize education in satellite countries.

Chapter 2

Totalitarian Nature of the Soviet World

What Are Soviets?

THE RUSSIAN word "soviet" means simply council. The first soviet was formed spontaneously in the Russian revolution of 1905 and consisted of representatives of anti-Czarist political parties and of unions and other working class organizations; in the countryside, it also included peasants.

Subsequently, Lenin defined soviets as "organs of insurrection . . . organs of revolutionary power." After the establishment of Soviet Russia, they were redefined as "the state form of the dictatorship of the proletariat." They were organized on a hierarchical and centralized basis, exercising both legislative and executive functions, with the Supreme Soviet at the apex of the governmental power structure. Under the Stalin Constitution, soviets are essentially legislative in function.

However, under both Lenin and Stalin, as well as under Khrushchev, the soviets have only been, as Lenin's doctrine specified they should be, "transmission belts" connecting the Communist Party with the population. They were "conductors of the general line of the Party."

How Is the Government Selected in the Soviet World?

Nominally, by elections. But the only candidates are Communist Party nominees or candidates put up by blocs consisting of the Communist Party and organizations controlled by it. The elections are not free and the outcome is predetermined.

Who Runs the Government in the Soviet World?

The government is run by the Communist Party. All important posts are held by communists. The most important positions are held by members of the Presidium.

The Soviet Presidium rules the U.S.S.R. and its satellites. While Stalin was alive, he was the acknowledged leader of the Presidium and of the Soviet empire. Stalin, whose real name was Yosif Djugashvili, was an old Bolshevik who joined Lenin's party before the Russian Revolution. During World War II, he assumed the premiership of the U.S.S.R. His power was greater than that of most rulers in history. He decided all important (and a vast number of lesser) questions. His decisions were considered infallible, and there was no appeal from them.

At the historic Twentieth Party Congress of the CPSU in February, 1956, Khrushchev, in his famous "secret report," condemned this entire mode of tyrannical leadership, which he called "the cult of personality." This cult consisted of two related phenomena: one-man dictatorship and widespread adulation of that one man. Khrushchev countered with what he proposed as the only proper means by which the Party and government were to be ruled: "collective leadership."

Thus, in the first three years after Stalin's death, many people in the West and behind the Iron Curtain were deceived into believing that collective leadership (a) was a new doctrine and (b) had actually been put into practice by Stalin's heirs.

The fact is that both Lenin and Stalin had glorified the notion of collective leadership; and Stalin especially always took pains to affirm that he was speaking not in his own name but in the name of the collective leadership. This theme was particularly prominent during the first few years after Lenin's death, at the very time that Stalin was craftily intriguing and maneuvering to get rid of the "collective leadership." Under cover of that formula Stalin destroyed the political power and status of his peers and betters in that collective leadership—Trotsky, Zinoviev, Kamenev, Bukharin, and many, many others—on his road to absolute tyranny. And later he physically liquidated them.

It was during a comparable period—the period of struggle for succession after Stalin's death in 1953—that his heirs, especially Khrushchev revived the same theme, at the very time when he was in process of destroying the political power and standing of his peers in the "collective leadership." In the years since he has gotten rid of all potential rivals, just as Stalin did—Beria, Bulganin, Malenkov, Kaganovitch, Molotov, Zhukov, and many others. He has not yet physically liquidated them. Neither did Stalin with *his* peers during the comparable period. And Khrushchev may never do so because such bloodletting is no longer necessary.

But in the very speech in which he condemned Stalin in 1956, Khrushchev explicitly reaffirmed the doctrinal basis on which Stalin himself had gone about his bloody purge business. And today, no less than before, the doctrine of a war against any and all opposition elements is bolstered by laws which permit it, and by the existence of the secret police.

By the same token, Khrushchev, in destroying the cult of Stalin's personality, created a vacuum which a totalitarian society must needs fill; and it has indeed been filled by the ever-growing adulation of Khrushchev, his personality, ideas and policies.

Do Freedom of Speech, Press, and Assembly Exist in the Soviet World?

All constitutions in the Soviet world "guarantee" civil liberties. But in practice civil liberties are non-existent.

All media of mass communication are in the hands of the government. The contents of all publications and public speeches must conform to official policy. Conformity is insured by censorship and severe punishment for deviation.

Do Writers, Artists, and Scientists Have Freedom of Expression in the Soviet World?

No. In the communist view, "art is a class weapon" and so is science. Art and science must serve the interests of the state.

The general function of art is to extol life in the Soviet

world; the general function of science is to develop methods for building up the Soviet world.

The communist party and the secret police are the final judges of artistic questions and scientific problems.

Individual works of art and the work of scientists are judged by their service to state policy. What was once approved because it fulfilled a need of the state, may later be officially condemned if the policy it served has been changed.

Artists, scholars, and scientists wear invisible uniforms in the service of the state. They are acclaimed, rewarded, criticized and purged in accordance with the shifting tides of state needs.

The casualties in the war of the Soviet state against the mind and spirit of man are legion.

Typical of the Stalinist attitude toward science and culture was the settlement of a dispute among biologists by the politicians of the Central Committee of the Bolshevik Party. These politicians pronounced correct the new theory of T. Lysenko that personality and cultural characteristics acquired through environmental influences could be inherited. At that time, it did not bother the central committee that all reputable biologists in the rest of the world had arrived through sound experimental evidence at a contrary conclusion. What the central committee was interested in was that Lysenko's "theory" could be used in support of the party's goal of remaking man in the image of Marxist theory.

Therefore, the teaching of formal genetics was forbidden. A purge of textbooks, scientific works, instructors, and scientists was carried out. A science was murdered and the secret police took its quota of victims for slave labor.

What Was the "Thaw"?

Along with the general decrease of terror and the easing of conditions of life that accompanied the insecurity of Stalin's heirs during their struggle for the succession, there came what was known as a "thaw" in Soviet cultural life.

It took its name from a short novel by Ilya Ehrenburg, always a literary bellwether of Soviet cultural policies. In effect, this novel, and the short two-year period that took its name from it, appeared to call for a greater degree of freedom from party control in cultural and literary matters.

The period reached its height in 1956. Its outside limits were defined by the publication of the book, *Not By Bread Alone,* by Vladimir Dudintsev. Regardless of its artistic merits, it was a mild, though genuine, attempt to go beyond the traditional themes of glorification of communism and the Soviet state to which writers had had to confine themselves. In this novel, the author actually portrayed a party official who was guilty of bureaucratic excesses; against this villain he counterposed a hero who had some original ideas which the villain in part squashed and in part took over. Criticism of Soviet life did not go beyond this; the Soviet system itself continued to be glorified.

Since all publication in the U.S.S.R. is official, the appearance of this novel and the reappearance in print of a number of older writers who had been silent for years, was taken as a measure of the new regime's greater leniency. The picture was blurred, however, by the fact that other official organs began to criticize Dudintsev and the other writers. It was all indicative of the relative confusion that existed at the time, stemming from the absence of a clear-cut policy at the top.

By 1957, however, the dust had begun to settle in the Kremlin leadership, and, in addition, it had learned the lesson taught by the 1956 revolutions in Poland and Hungary, of allowing writers and intellectuals too much leeway. In that direction lay danger for the one-party state. The lid had been taken off for a short while in the Soviet world. After 1957 it was put back on tightly. The "thaw" had ended. No better illustration of this fact can be found than the treatment given to the Soviet author, Boris Pasternak (who died of natural causes at the age of 70 in May, 1960).

What Was the Pasternak Case?

Pasternak, a pioneer figure in Soviet poetry of the 1920s and 1930s, wrote a novel, *Doctor Zhivago,* which was refused publication in the U.S.S.R. because of its clear non-communist political and artistic attitudes. The manuscript found its way secretly to Italy, where a leading publisher brought it out in translation; soon thereafter it appeared in English and other languages. (By 1960, it had still not appeared inside the Soviet Union.)

The novel, though it had its literary detractors in the West, was generally acclaimed as a masterpiece and Pasternak was awarded the Nobel Prize for literature in 1958. This event served to unleash a torrent of the most violent criticism of Pasternak in the entire Soviet press; he was likened to a dog and a pig, and was forbidden to travel to Sweden to receive his prize. In turn, a worldwide protest arose in the West against the treatment accorded Pasternak in his own country. He became a symbol of the free spirit in shackles.

What Is the State of Mind of Soviet Literary Creators Today?

For many years, the most gifted and sensitive of the Soviet poets, novelists and dramatists either were silent or wrote "for the drawer"—secretly, or only for the intimacy of family and trusted friends. The literary hacks, of course, made their way nicely by conforming to the party line for literature. All except the most callous were consumed with one or another form of guilt at their silence or complicity in the terror exercised during the Stalin years against many fellow writers and intellectuals, among all the rest of the Russian people. The death of Stalin, and Khrushchev's sensational "secret speech" of 1956, leading to the thaw, produced a sense of relief, but in the end only confusion as to the narrow limits of relief from the party straitjacket in literature.

Today the confusion persists. Much writing "for the drawer" continues. Increasingly, the more daring of the younger writers smuggle out poems, stories, even short novels, which reflect their confusion, their sense of isolation from Western culture, their awareness of their humiliation as men of letters in what is still a rigid, bureaucratic, totalitarian society. But above all they reveal (especially the young writers) that their spirit, their thrust to free expression in a free society, has not been destroyed. Such themes, or at least muted consideration of themes related to them, even occasionally peep out in some of the literary material that is now being published in the Soviet Union. After nearly half a century of repression, the hidden and semi-secret drives of the best Soviet writers show that the spirit of man cannot be downed permanently.

The official journals of the literary associations, bound as they are to the dictates of party and government, continue to reflect the same cowardly obsequiousness to the regime that has always characterized the party press in the U.S.S.R. Two recent examples demonstrate this—and reveal at the same time that the "cult of personality," so condemned by Khrushchev when applied to Stalin, is now being increasingly exercised toward him.

Some 10 months ago, Khrushchev made a speech to the Soviet intellectuals which was first published in the spring of 1961. In that address, the Soviet dictator indicated that the absolute rigidity of the Stalinist rule of literature would not return, though he warned that he would exercise the "right of leadership" to criticize and condemn when a writer had stepped too far. Nevertheless, the tenor of the speech was relaxed and the writers got the assurance of more flexibility. The publication of the speech was followed by a spate of obsequious tributes of which two are cited here:

"One cannot read the speech of N. S. Khrushchev without a feeling of joyous excitement. There is so much love in it for literature and writers, so much concern about the flourishing of the arts. One reads Comrade Khrushchev and it seems that the heart itself says, 'Many thanks to our great friend, Nikita Sergeyevich.' "

(*Literature and Life*, May 19, 1961)

"The words of the great contemporary humanist reveal the very essence of Soviet literature. . . . The words of N. S. Khrushchev give wings to Soviet writers, bring light to many literary problems. They are full of fatherly confidence and by wise and good counsel they direct us toward the solution of our main problems. . . ."

(*Literary Gazette,* May 13, 1961)

What Is the Role of Education in the Soviet World?

"Education in the U.S.S.R.," reads *Pedagogy,* a textbook approved in 1946 by the Soviet government for use in training teachers, "is a weapon for strengthening the Soviet state and the building of a classless society."

"The Soviet schools cannot be satisfied to rear merely educated persons but should instill the ideology of communism in the mind of the young generation, shape a Marxist-Leninist world outlook and inculcate the spirit of Soviet patriotism and Bolshevik ideas," declared the publication *Cultural Life* in August, 1947.

The schools, dictates *Pedagogy,* must turn out "organization-minded and disciplined" people full of "love of our Motherland . . . and of our glorious Communist Party and its leaders . . ."

These precepts also govern education in the satellite states.

Under this system, the Communist Party is the formulator of educational policy which is continuously revised in accordance with the changing needs of the regime.

The lower schools are instruments of indoctrination and propaganda; institutions of higher learning are Communist Party seminars. The courts are, in effect, catechisms in communist ideology.

History is continually rewritten and textbooks revised as the communists falsify past and present in accordance with the changing needs of their strategic situation. Thus, for example, after Beria's execution all mention of his name was excised from communist encyclopedias.

Critical attitudes and free inquiry are forbidden.

". . . objectivism and the impartial assembling of economic facts is inadmissible," said the publication

Bolshevik. In 1947, *Cultural Life* declared the "spirit of political indifference, impartiality and academic neutrality" are "impermissible" and result in "the distortion of historical truth."

Academic freedom does not exist. Public education, however, is free.

Though these basic doctrines of education were formulated in the Stalin era, they have been reiterated forcefully by Khrushchev, and by the party leaders in all the satellites.

In 1959, wholesale administrative and organizational modifications were made in the Soviet school system. Their fundamental import, however, was only to re-emphasize the trend and direction of Soviet education until then.

The system has several aims. The universities and other institutions of higher learning are limited to the admission of some 450,000 freshmen a year. Of these, fully 95% are channeled into technical, scientific and mathematical studies, leaving only 5% for art, literature, classics and the other humanities.

In turn, the secondary schools are geared to this system. The emphasis is overwhelmingly on the technical and practical sides.

In addition, preference is given, both in the secondary system and in higher education, to students who have put in at least two years of practical labor in agriculture or industry. Arrangements are variously made for secondary and university students either to work evenings, weekends and vacations, or for a full two-year period upon graduation.

The emphasis in the secondary schools is thus on vocational studies and applied science.

This is accompanied by the restriction of the further growth of full-time universities, in favor of the expansion of part-time higher education.

The end result, in Khrushchev's terms, is to produce a younger generation that will take its place in the physical construction of an industrially strong Soviet Union. In terms of higher educational goals as they have been understood in the West, this system is geared to produce technically competent, but ill-educated and half-cultured, citizens.

Do Inhabitants of the Soviet World Have
Freedom of Movement?

Travel between the U.S.S.R. and its satellites and among the satellites is strictly controlled.

In the U.S.S.R., as in Tsarist Russia, internal passports are required for travel.

After completion of their sentences, certain categories of political offenders are not permitted to reside in the larger cities and administrative centers of the country.

Do Inhabitants of the Soviet World Have
Inviolability of Their Persons and Homes?

Constitutionally, yes. In practice, no.

Under Stalin, the power of the secret police was supreme. People disappeared suddenly from their accustomed places of work and homes and were never heard from again. Like the plagues of old, purges carried off millions to prisons, slave labor and death. At one time, shortly before Stalin's death, the number of slave laborers in the forced labor camps was reliably estimated to be 20,000,000.

Since Stalin's death, this system of terror has seriously diminished. But, for example, the right of habeas corpus still does not exist in the U.S.S.R. In the course of a series of amnesties in 1955 and 1957, large numbers of prisoners were released. But the forced labor camps remain, the secret police remains, political prisoners have not been amnestied to the same degree as actual criminals, and it is estimated that some 3,000,000 still remain imprisoned in the camps.

What Is the Nature of Law in the Soviet World?

In the Soviet social system, the interests of the individual are subservient to the interests of the state. The distinction between private and public law, prevalent throughout the rest of the world, is rejected. In practice, the difference between government policy and law is thin or non-existent.

The primary function of Soviet law is the suppression of all private rights, the regimentation and subordination of the individual to the state and the creation of a totalitarian state.

The primary concern of the law in the Soviet world is what is known there as "socialist legality," which was defined by the late Andrei Vishinsky, former Foreign Minister, Chief Public Prosecutor and author of the official Soviet law text, as "the subordination of the formal commands of law to those of the Communist Party policy."

This situation has remained unchanged from Stalin's day to Khrushchev's.

What Is the Role of the Courts in the Soviet World?

Theoretically the courts in the Soviet system are set up for the fair trial and sentencing of offenders. However, they are not independent of other branches of the government, as in the United States, but are regarded as instruments of state policy.

No decisions adverse to state policy are ever made by the judges. The outcome of trials involving important economic and political issues is predetermined by the Presidium. Virtually all judges are communists.

In the Soviet world, trials are often staged for propaganda purposes to support the domestic and foreign policies of the government.

In the purge trials of 1935-1939 in the U.S.S.R., when the policy of the Soviet government was anti-fascist, the defendants were accused of treason and spying on behalf of Germany.

In the trials held in the satellite states during the "cold war," the defendants were accused of spying on behalf of "Anglo-American imperialism."

What Was the MVD?

Until shortly after Stalin's death and the execution of Beria, the MVD, successor to the NKVD, OGPU, GPU, and Cheka, was the secret police of the U.S.S.R. What follows is a brief description of what its duties were and how it carried them out. This description is given here because, though many of the worst features of terror which characterized the secret police regime have been eliminated, the secret police continues to exist. And though its existence is more shadowy than it ever was under Stalin, the rules under which it operates remain substantially on the books.

The MVD's chief function was to insure blind obedience through terrorism. Stalin characterized it as "the unsheathed sword of the revolution."

The MVD had vast powers. It was frequently described as a state within a state. It had its own independent budget within the general state budget. It maintained its own armed forces, including air, tank and infantry divisions. (Since Stalin's death, its budget has been subjected to the control of the Soviet Council of Ministers; similarly, its armed forces have largely been transferred to the Ministry of Defense.)

Secret police forces still guard the borders of the U.S.S.R. Under Stalin's tyranny, it rounded up for deportation to Siberia and northern Russia "politically unreliable" population groups, as well as millions of other suspected citizens.

The MVD spied on the entire population. It kept watch over all officials and representatives of the Party and state, and over economic, social and cultural institutions. It also watched over the officers of the Soviet armed forces. These functions are retained, more discreetly, by the secret police today.

Among the most dreaded powers of the MVD were summary arrest and indefinite detention; imposition of sentence by decree in the absence of the defendant; prolonged interrogation and torture in the extraction of confessions; secret trials of "enemies of the people," that is, persons accused of political crimes; and secret executions. The secret police no longer practices these.

The MVD was the recruiting agency for the slave-labor industries, and it administered the slave labor camps. These functions the secret police still retain.

The MVD also kept careful watch over the communist movement outside the U.S.S.R. and of the satellite governments. The secret police today still have this function.

What Is the KGB?

The KGB—the Committee for State Security—is the successor to the MVD. It is headed by General Ivan Serov, the shadowy figure who supervised the forcible annexation of Latvia, Lithuania and Estonia to the U.S.S.R. in 1940, and who was in charge of the brutal suppression of the Hungarian Revolution in 1956.

Though the Soviet regime under Khrushchev is clearly more humane than was Stalin's, under his one-party totalitarian state, the secret police is, as Merle Fainsod, one of the most distinguished students of Soviet society and government, has put it, "ready for use when needed, operative, above all, even when not visible, by the mere fact that it is known to exist."

Do Inhabitants of the Soviet World
Enjoy Freedom of Worship?

No. This, however, does not prevent communists outside the Soviet world, when it suits their purpose, from posing as pious religious believers—whether it is as Catholics in Italy, or as Moslems in the Arab world.

A similar flexibility in tactics characterizes communist policy toward religion behind the Iron Curtain. Soviet constitutions "guarantee" freedom of religious worship and freedom from anti-religious propaganda. Between this nicely balanced phraseology and the reality of communist policy, however, there are wide discrepancies.

Following the Bolshevik revolution of 1917, the Soviet government began a systematic persecution of the Orthodox Church, which for centuries, under the Tsars, had been the only recognized religious body in Russia. When Stalin became absolute master of the Soviet state, and the state became a totalitarian autocracy, Stalin revived the old Tsarist pattern of state and church relationships. He acquired full control of the church, and the church became an instrument of the state. During World War II, atheist publications were discontinued, while priests accompanied troops to the front. While the legal position of the church has been restored and it enjoys greater latitude than in the first years of the Soviet Union, religious schools, societies and parishes are still forbidden. Every church building is required to display a Red flag, and when Stalin was alive, a picture or icon of him.

After the war, the Soviet state established the supremacy of the Russian church over the Orthodox churches in the satellite countries. Thus was forged another weapon for control of the Soviet empire. It also aided Soviet religious and political maneuvers among people of the Orthodox faith in lands beyond the Iron Curtain, notably the Near East.

What Is Communist Policy Toward Religion in the Satellite Countries?

The principal element in communist policy toward religion in the satellite countries is the drive of the state to obtain control of the church and make it subservient to the government.

Although all churches in the satellite states suffer under the impact of ruthless communist persecution, world public attention has centered on the conflict between these governments and the Catholic Church. The Orthodox churches have been taken over, and Protestant influence is only a minor factor. But the Roman Catholic Church, with its widespread educational system, its world center in Rome, and its enormous influence on world public opinion, proved a formidable opponent. Despite its serious losses and weakened position, the Catholic Church in the satellite countries remains a center of resistance to communist power.

An outstanding example of such effective resistance, supported by the people, is the situation in Poland. There Gomulka has realized, since he came to power in October, 1956, that he could not renew the traditional communist onslaught on the Catholic Church without incurring the wrath and disloyalty of the vast majority of the people. The Church, for its part, has staunchly defended its minimal prerogatives, secure in the knowledge of popular support. Thus, an uneasy quasi-alliance was formed between Gomulka and Cardinal Wyszynski, the head of the Church in Poland.

Though the regime from time to time engages in fitful incursions into the Church's realm, by and large the faithful are allowed to practice their religion with a considerable degree of freedom. The Church, in turn, does not preach overt or violent resistance to the regime; both sides want peace, each for its own reasons—Gomulka because he needs it to keep his regime from the devastations of even a muted civil war, the Church because it believes that so long as it retains the loyalty of the faithful it will outlast communism.

Is Communism Compatible with Religion?

No. Communism and religion are irreconcilable. Communism, in theory and practice, is atheistic. It regards religion, in the well-known phrase of Marx, as "the opium of the people."

The Judaeo-Christian tradition treats each man as being individually important. Communism does the exact opposite—it treats man as an instrument of the state. "All phrases about equal rights are nonsense." (Lenin.) This basically anti-religious statement is opposed to the Bible's precept that to deprive a man of his freedom is considered equivalent to murder. (Exodus 21:16.)

Few enemies of Judaeo-Christian ethics have been as unashamed as the communists in expressing their own amoral philosophy. "Communist ethics make it the highest duty to accept the necessity of acting wickedly . . . Evil transforms itself into good through the dialectic of History." (George Lukacs, Commissar of Education in the post-World War I Bolshevik government of Hungary.) This is in direct contrast to one of the basic tenets of the Judaeo-Christian tradition. The Talmud, for instance, says that "a good deed performed by means of a sin is invalid."

Thus, no truly religious person, whether Christian or Jew, can possibly accept communism. A doctrine which believes that "To us everything is permitted" (Lenin) is totally irreconcilable with one which requires of its adherents that "Thou shalt love thy neighbor as thyself." (Leviticus 19:18.)

How Are National Minorities Treated in the Soviet World?

Communist propaganda boasts that only in the Soviet world are national minorities free of oppression. The record belies the propaganda.

The philosophy governing Soviet national minorities policy is based on the doctrine enunciated by Stalin in the late 1920s. It was put in capsule form by the party propagandists: "National in form, socialist in content." In theory, this meant that the more than 200 distinct nationalities and ethnic minorities would be able to hold on to their cultural-ethnic traditions, so long as they supported Marxist-Leninist ideology and the Soviet state. This doctrine should have meant that all these minority cultures would be able to flourish.

In practice, the opposite has been true. "National in form" has remained an empty formula; "socialist in content" became the order of the day. It meant that the newspapers, schools, books, party and state organs in the various national republics and autonomous regions of the U.S.S.R. became carbon copies of their Russian counterparts, exactly aping in their own languages the formulae of Moscow.

During the war years, Stalin abolished a number of the so-called autonomous republics by decree. He had "politically unreliable" population groups—millions of Volga Germans, Poles, Letts, Estonians, Lithuanians, Crimean Tartars, Greeks from the Black Sea region of the U.S.S.R., East Germans, and such smaller nationality groups as the Caspian Kalmucks, the Chechens, Ingush and Balkars—forcibly uprooted from their homes and transported under inhuman conditions to remote regions for slave labor. Strategic border regions were repopulated with Russians and other population groups considered politically reliable.

Though Khrushchev, in his 1956 "secret report," condemned Stalin for *some* of these crimes (in a few cases amounting to genocide), he was silent about most of these policies. And in any event, the Soviet regime has done little or nothing to redress the injustice to these groups.

The oppression of national minorities is also a practice of the satellites.

What Is Birobidjan?

In the late 1920s, the Soviet government initiated on the Siberian-Chinese border the Jewish settlement of the province of Birobidjan. As stated officially, it was to be an agricultural settlement for urban Jews. Its unstated purpose was to counteract the large number of Chinese who had been infiltrating the province.

In the early years, only 30,000 Jews immigrated to the harsh climate of Birobidjan, and in order to attract greater numbers, the Soviet propaganda machine began hailing the area as a new national homeland for the Soviet Jews. This had no pronounced effect on immigration to the area, however. By 1948, with the rise of official sentiment against the Jews, the policy of the government was reversed. All Jewish schools and publications were closed down and a purge of Jewish leaders was carried out in 1949-50.

Estimates as to the present size of the Jewish population of Birobidjan vary. Some authorities place it as low as 40,000. The Jews in that area constitute 25 per cent of the territory's inhabitants, the rest consisting of Tartars, Ukrainians, and Russians. After a quarter of a century of settlement in this "Jewish territory," no cultural Jewish institutions of any kind are left. There is neither a Jewish school nor a Jewish theatre, but only one dilapidated synagogue without a rabbi. As late as 1960 a Jewish newspaper with a circulation of 1,000 was issued three times a week; however, this paper does little more than parrot official news rehashed from the official Moscow newspapers, *Pravda* and *Izvestia*.

What Is the Background of the Status of the Jews in the Soviet Union?

For about three decades very little came to light about the real situation of Jews in the Soviet Union. The world took at face value the Soviet legal code's definition of anti-Semitism as a crime. No special importance was attached to the indifference with which the Soviet government, in common with other governments, watched first the persecution and then the extermination of the Jews in Hitler's Germany. The borders of the "socialist fatherland" were not opened to Jews.

Following the partition of Poland by Hitler and Stalin, the Soviet government barred the escape of hundreds of thousands of Jews fleeing eastward before the onrushing Nazi hordes. And it deported hundreds of thousands of Jews from its own "sphere of influence" in Poland to slave labor in the interior of the U.S.S.R.

What Has Happened to Jewish Institutions in the U.S.S.R.?

After World War II, the position of Soviet Jews deteriorated rapidly. Jewish schools were closed. The teaching of Yiddish and Hebrew was discontinued. All Jewish organizations were dissolved and all periodicals and publications dealing with Jewish problems were suppressed. A purge of Jewish intellectuals was carried out. Relations between Soviet Jews, who were warned not to identify themselves with Israel, and Jewish communities in other parts of the world, were forbidden. Large numbers of Jews were forcibly deported for slave labor in the interior of Russia.

All of this happened in Stalin's last years, from 1948 to 1953, which were known throughout the Soviet Jewish community of 3,000,000 as the "Black Years."

Though the violence, and the threat of even more of it, ended with Stalin's death, no change has occurred in the status of Soviet Jewry: official Soviet facts and figures reveal a pattern of anti-Jewish policies, of differential treatment in cultural and religious affairs, of discrimination in education and government employment, of denigration of the Jew's social image, of scarcely concealed anti-Semitic prejudices.

What Is the Status of Jewish Culture in the U.S.S.R.?

Once the matrix of much of Jewish culture, the great Soviet Jewish community, from late 1948 to the mid 1960's, was utterly deprived of any means to express itself in creative terms. Yiddish writers could have some of their manuscripts published in Russian translation, but were not allowed to publish in their own language, for Yiddish publishing houses were forbidden. So were the Yiddish press, theatre, schools, newspapers and every other aspect of organized Jewish culture. In the late 1950's, a few minor concessions were made to the Soviet Jewish community; some concerts of Yiddish songs were permitted, and the Kremlin allowed publication of a few secular Yiddish books. In 1961, the Kremlin allowed still another concession—the establishment of a bimonthly literary review.

How Was Anti-Semitism Officially Expressed Under Stalin?

There is no such thing as an independent journal in the Soviet Union. Everything published in the U.S.S.R. for popular consumption is rigidly controlled by the state, and every opinion expressed in a newspaper is equivalent to an official opinion. It is therefore interesting to note that both *Culture and Life* and the *Literary Gazette,* leading cultural periodicals of the U.S.S.R., initiated in 1949 an editorial policy which effectively brought the real government attitude toward the Jews into the open.

In articles dealing with "pernicious" western influences which had been "contaminating" Soviet literature, both publications listed a large number of writers who were suspect. In each case the Jewish writers whose pen names appeared on this list were additionally identified by their original names, all of which were immediately identifiable as of Jewish origin. Interestingly enough, the magazines did not find it necessary to supply the original names of the non-Jewish writers. But the full extent of communist anti-Semitism was revealed in the Prague show trials and in the so-called "doctor's plot."

During the month of November, 1952, the Czech communists staged a mammoth show trial. Eleven of the fourteen defendants were Jews, all of them veteran communists. They included the Secretary General of the Czech Communist Party, Rudolph Slansky; the editor of the communist newspaper *Rude Pravo,* Andre Simone; and nine other officials in various government departments. The most significant aspect of the trial was the fact that the defendants were tried not as individuals, but as Jews. They were accused of being agents of a world-wide "Jewish bourgeois nationalistic plot." They were forced to confess that they had become traitors and conspirators because of their Jewish bourgeois origin. Although all their lives they had been violent opponents of Zionism, they were forced to admit that they had acted for the benefit of the Zionist movement. Even the three non-Jewish defendants, including the former Foreign Minister Clementis, "confessed" as their main crime that they had placed "Zionist agents" in their offices.

The defendants also had to accept the blame for food rationing, lack of bread, lack of electricity, continued low wages and high prices, and the failure of government plans. A fantastic treason charge linked them with an imaginary spy net masterminded by U. S. President Harry Truman, U. S. Secretary of State Dean Acheson, Israel Premier David Ben-Gurion, Israeli Foreign Minister Moshe Sharett and U. S. Secretary of the Treasury Henry Morgenthau, Jr.

These "legal" procedures were accompanied by anti-Semitic outbursts in the press of a virulence unknown in the history of Czechoslovakia. When, on December 4, 1952, the trial ended with the hanging of 11 of the 14 accused, the myth of communist tolerance of minorities was shattered even for the most gullible.

One month later, nine doctors, most of them Jews, were seized in Moscow on the charge of plotting against prominent government leaders. Again the trial was accompanied by outspoken anti-Semitic editorials in the Moscow press. During the trial the accused "admitted" all charges, including killing the late Andrei Zhdanov.

After Stalin's death, in a sudden turn-about, the "guilty" men were completely exonerated, the plot declared fictitious and their "confessions" revealed to have been the result of torture.

How Is Anti-Semitism Officially Expressed Under Khrushchev?

There is a concerted propaganda campaign in the Soviet press and radio to single out Jews and Judaism for special opprobrium. This campaign began in earnest in 1957, with the general ending of the "thaw," and continued unabated thereafter. As of the middle of 1960, it remained at a high pitch of intensity.

This campaign follows a definite pattern. In one strand, the Jewish religion is denigrated and vilified; it is shown to be linked with the vicious twins of "bourgeois nationalism" and Zionism, both of which are intimately associated with "Western imperialism and its Israeli puppet."

A second strand perpetuates the traditional anti-Semitic stereotypes of Jews as anti-social types.

The two together create an image of the Jews and Judaism as virtually disloyal and potentially treasonous to the Soviet state.

What Is the Status of the Jewish Religion in the U.S.S.R.?

Communism is militantly atheistic in ideology and practice and all religious groups are seriously disadvantaged in the Soviet Union. But even in religion the Jews are singled out for discriminatory treatment.

They are allowed no Chief Rabbi and, unlike the other religious groups, no central, nation-wide organization of religious congregations.

There are very few rabbis, and the number of students in the one rabbinical seminary that is permitted is kept down to about 20. Many communities are forbidden to have synagogues, or even to have damaged synagogues repaired. In many communities, synagogues have actually been closed down by police force, private prayer meetings forbidden, and many religious practices, such as the baking of matzos and ritual slaughter of animals for kosher food consumption, prohibited.

What Is the Soviet Attitude Toward Zionism?

In classic communist doctrine, Zionism is a "counter-revolutionary movement of the Jewish bourgeoisie," which divides the working class along nationalist lines and imperils their revolutionary unity. Zionism has long been persecuted in the U.S.S.R. In Palestine the communists incited pogroms by the Arabs against the Jews.

However, during the struggle of the Jews against the British in Palestine after World War II, the Soviet satellites encouraged emigration to Israel, in order to weaken British power in the Near East. The Soviet Union, however, prevented emigration of "its" Jews.

Subsequently, when the state of Israel was created, and resisted Soviet domination, Soviet policy toward Zionism hardened again.

What Is the Soviet Attitude Toward Israel?

The Soviet regime is violently hostile to Israel for two reasons: foreign policy and domestic policy.

Its foreign policy in the Middle East dictates a close relationship with the Arab countries, and this has led the U.S.S.R. to demonstrate its hatred for Israel both in terms of propaganda and in terms of enormous military aid to build up the Arab armed forces.

Domestically, the Soviet need to present Israel in the worst possible light is based on the official assumption of the alien, hostile and suspect character of its Jewish citizens and on the concomitant conviction that Israel would serve as a magnet to attract Soviet Jews. In consequence, the Soviet press is full of vitriolic denunciations of Israel, of its way of life and conditions of living, and of its alleged alliance with the "imperialists."

What Has Happened to Jewish Institutions in the Satellite Countries?

The bulk of the 6,000,000 Jews who were slaughtered by the Nazis during World War II lived in the countries that subsequently became Soviet satellites. After the war, the remnants of those communities slowly began to rebuild their communal and cultural institutions. This painful process was cut short soon after the communists attained power in the satellites.

Generally, throughout the satellites, all formerly independent Jewish religious, educational and social activities have been nationalized and are operated by communist party members or have been abolished. All Jewish political parties have been dissolved. The number of Jewish schools is dwindling. In some countries the teaching of Hebrew is forbidden. In Hungary, Jewish teachers have been ousted from the public school system and Jewish pupils are compelled to attend school on the Sabbath.

Jewish charity organizations, including orphanages, children's homes and hospitals have been liquidated. Jewish foreign relief organizations have been ousted. Jewish papers are permitted to publish only communist views. Government spies sit in the synagogues, many of which have been invaded and desecrated.

Anti-Semitic attacks by communist cabinet members were not uncommon in Hungary, where pogroms took place in the winter of 1950-51. Hungarian Jews and others "dangerous to the security of the State" were deported for forced labor.

In recent years, the situation of the Jews in the satellites has fluctuated, but it is evidently in better condition than under the worst of the Stalinist tyranny. In Poland, for example, the communist-controlled Jewish community is allowed a daily Yiddish newspaper. And Jews have been allowed to emigrate, from time to time, from both Poland and Rumania.

In these respects, these Jewish communities are better off than Soviet Jewry itself.

Bibliography

Blake, Patricia and Hayward, Max, editors
DISSONANT VOICES IN SOVIET LITERATURE,
Partisan Review magazine, 1961.
> A special double issue of the well-known New
> York literary journal covering a period of 43
> years of Soviet writing.

FACTS: Reports on organized anti-Semitism, Vol. 13,
No. 11
ANTI-JEWISH PROPAGANDA IN THE SOVIET
UNION, Anti-Defamation League of B'nai B'rith,
October, 1960.
> An examination of Soviet press attacks in re-
> cent years against Jews, Judaism and Israel.

Fainsod, Merle
HOW RUSSIA IS RULED, Harvard University Press,
1953.
> The best systematic account of the structure and
> institutions of Soviet rule.

Goldberg, B. Z.
THE JEWISH PROBLEM IN THE SOVIET UNION,
Crown, 1961.
> An analysis based on many years of close observa-
> tion and three extended visits to the U.S.S.R.

House of Representatives, 83rd Congress, 2nd Session,
1954.
TREATMENT OF JEWS BY THE SOVIET. Sev-
enth Interim Report of Hearings Before the Select
Committee on Communist Aggression, House of
Representatives, Eighty-Third Congress. United
States Government Printing Office, Washington,
1954.
> Expert testimony on racial persecution in Rus-
> sia and the satellites.

Lyons, Eugene
OUR SECRET ALLIES, Duell, Sloan and Pearce,
1950.
> The struggle of the Russian people against the
> regime, told by a veteran observer.

Markham, R. H.
COMMUNISTS CRUSH CHURCHES IN EASTERN EUROPE, Meador Publishing Co., 1950.
>   The destruction of religion and religious life in Eastern Europe under Soviet domination.

Meyer, Peter, *et al.*
THE JEWS IN THE SOVIET SATELLITES, Syracuse University Press, 1953.
>   An authoritative expose of Jewish persecution in Soviet satellites.

Milosz, Czeslaw
THE CAPTIVE MIND, A. Knopf, 1953.
>   Intellectual life under the Soviets.

The New Leader (a weekly publication)
JEWS IN THE SOVIET UNION, New York, September 14, 1959.
>   A documentary report by the editors.

Novak, Joseph
THE FUTURE IS OURS, COMRADE, Doubleday & Co., 1960.
>   Conversations with the Russians on Soviet ideals and life.

Pipes, Richard
THE FORMATION OF THE SOVIET UNION, Harvard University Press, 1954.
>   A study, by a leading authority, of Soviet national minorities policies.

Pipes, Richard, editor
THE RUSSIAN INTELLIGENTSIA, Columbia University Press, 1961.
>   A wide range of authoritative opinion on the intellectual life in Tsarist and Soviet Russia.

Problems of Communism, Volume X, No. 3, May-June 1961.
>   This issue of the highly informative bi-monthly magazine issued by the United States Information Agency contains an illuminating section on the state of mind of present-day Soviet intellectuals and literary people.

Schwarz, Solomon M.
THE JEWS IN THE SOVIET UNION, Syracuse University Press, 1951.
Soviet policy toward minorities, and anti-Semitism in the U.S.S.R.

Simmon, E. J.
THROUGH THE GLASS OF SOVIET LITERATURE, Columbia University Press, 1953.
Government controls and its effects on the intellectual life.

Steinberg, Julien
VERDICT OF THREE DECADES, Duell, Sloan and Pearce, 1950.
Traces the intellectual development of communism over three decades.

Struve, Gleb P.
SOVIET RUSSIAN LITERATURE: 1917-1950, University of Oklahoma Press, 1951.
A scholarly history up till 1950.

Teller, Judd L.
THE KREMLIN, THE JEWS AND THE MIDDLE EAST, Yoseloff Inc., 1957.
Describes Soviet policy toward their own Jews and the Israelis.

Timasheff, N. S.
RELIGION IN SOVIET RUSSIA, Sheed and Ward, 1942.
The relation between church and state in Russia, and the status of the different religions in the U.S.S.R.

Wolfe, Bertram D.
SIX KEYS TO THE SOVIET SYSTEM, Beacon Press, 1956.
An analysis of the permanencies of Soviet rule from Stalin through Khrushchev.

Zirkle, Conway
DEATH OF A SCIENCE IN RUSSIA, University of Pennsylvania Press, 1949.
The fate of the theory of genetics as described in Soviet publications.

Chapter 3

Economy and Labor in the Soviet World

Who Controls the Means of Production in the Soviet World?

IN THE U.S.S.R. all the principal means of production, exchange and distribution are "socialist property." Ownership and control are vested in the state.

In the satellite states and China, the transformation of private property into "socialist property" is not complete and is still in process.

In neither country can this system be called genuinely socialist—for "socialist property" is not in the hands of the people, or of elected representatives responsible to them. It is owned and controlled by the managerial state which is controlled by the party hierarchy.

What Were the Five-Year Plans?

The five-year plans, the first of a series of which was instituted by Stalin in 1929, were the "state national economic plans." They are regarded, in the Soviet world, as the principal factor in the transformation from the dictatorship of the proletariat to "socialism," and from "socialism" to communism.

What Is the Seven-Year Plan?

In 1959, Khrushchev and his colleagues announced a new economic plan to succeed the last of the Stalin five-year plans. This projected even more ambitious aspirations for the Soviet economy than any of its predecessors. It was projected for a period of seven years.

The plans provide for rapid industrialization and for collectivization and mechanization of agriculture. They aim at systematic exploitation of the vast resources of the Soviet world. The plans set production goals in each industry and plant, provide a standard for increasing production, set standards of quality, fix prices, and make allotments for wages and social services.

What Have Been the Results of Economic Planning in the U.S.S.R.?

The principal results of the five-year plans in the U.S.S.R. include:

Transformation of an economically backward country into the second greatest industrial nation of the world;

Increased urbanization of the population and creation of hundreds of new cities;

Increase in the size and proportion in the population of the working class;

Partial transformation of the peasant into a collective farmer and agricultural proletarian.

The incalculable human cost at which these material gains were made can only be guessed at in terms of the following:

Creation of a new class of 20 million slave laborers as an integral part of Soviet economy.

Expansion of the secret police to enforce compliance.

The uprooting and deportation of millions of peasants.

Creation of a new bureaucracy of party functionaries and military personnel.

Continued low standard of living for the majority of the people.

Under the Khrushchev seven-year plan, slave labor no longer plays an important role. This plan perpetuates the traditional Soviet emphasis on massive industrial expansion under state control and farm collectivization. It also promises better living conditions, in terms of increased housing and more and varied foods and clothing.

What Is the Position of the Peasant in the Soviet World?

Peasants comprise an overwhelming majority of the population of the Soviet world.

The peasant is the main target of the communist plan

of social development. The aim of communist policy is to transform the peasant into an agrarian worker. In the meantime, the peasant is the principal source of slave labor.

Peasant support of communism is won by land reform —the expropriation of large landholdings and their distribution among the peasants.

After a time, varying in length according to circumstances, the peasants are induced, coerced, or forced at gunpoint into collective farms where they work under state direction and control.

The production of the collectives is the property of the collectives. A fixed proportion is sold to the state at prices set by the state. Another portion is taken by the state in payment of various services and for various funds. The net income is distributed among the peasants of the collectives, partly in money, partly in kind, in proportion to the quantity and quality of their work, at rates determined by the state.

Collective farmers are permitted to cultivate crops and raise livestock on their own small garden plots. They are also permitted to dispose of a part of their private production on the open market.

Whenever, in consequence, peasant income rises, the state increases agricultural taxes. The revaluation of the ruble in 1947 was especially designed to decrease the value of the peasant's cash savings by 90%. The peasant in the Soviet world lives a life of drab poverty. On more than one occasion, famine, resulting from the perpetual antagonism between the state and the peasants in the U.S.S.R., has carried off millions of peasants. Millions more were driven from their homes to become slave laborers.

A growing number of state farms are operated by the government of the U.S.S.R. with agrarian workers who receive wages and are in fact agricultural proletarians.

What Is Labor's Standard of Living in the Soviet World?

It is apparent from the record of Soviet behavior that

the goal of the system is not primarily to better the life of the consumer, but to enhance the power of the state. Consumers receive improved benefits only as the rulers believe more goods or shorter hours will increase productivity and keep unrest within manageable limits.

The Statistical Office of the United Nations reported on December 3, 1950, on the basis of official reports, that with the exception of Poland, a Soviet satellite, the Soviet Union has the lowest per capita income of all industrialized and semi-industrialized nations of the world. National income per capita in the Soviet Union was equivalent to $308 a year in 1949 U. S. dollars.

A Bureau of Labor Statistics study estimated that in the spring of 1953 a Moscow worker had to work up to twenty-five times as much as a worker in New York to buy basic foods, and up to twenty times as much to buy basic clothing.

A 1957 study prepared by the Library of Congress for the Joint Economic Committee, on the subject of "Soviet Economic Growth," revealed that the per capita personal consumption in the Soviet Union is only about one-fifth to one-seventh as great as that in the United States.

Labor's income in the Soviet Union is lower than the national per capita average. In theory, a comprehensive system of social services supplements labor's income. In practice, the social services benefit only a minority of workers.

While the state concentrates on heavy industry and armaments, labor suffers from an acute and chronic shortage of housing and consumer goods.

Can a Worker Choose His Place of Work in the Soviet World?

Only within narrowing limits. Since 1940 the government of the Soviet Union has followed the practice of transferring skilled workers from plant to plant without regard to the workers' wishes.

The graduates of the Labor Reserve Schools are required to work for four years at the direction of the government.

Can a Worker Quit His Job in the Soviet World?

Only for reasons approved by the state, and only with the permission of his plant managers.

Leaving a job without permission is a criminal offense in the U.S.S.R. The punishment is imprisonment for two to four years.

Workers in the transportation industries work under martial law; those who leave their jobs without permission are tried by court martial and may be sentenced to prison for five to eight years.

How Are Lateness and Absenteeism by Workers Punished in the Soviet World?

In the U.S.S.R., a worker who is late more than twenty minutes three times in a month, or four times in two months, is considered unjustifiably absent. He may be sentenced to as much as six months' compulsory labor at his regular place of employment and, during the period of his sentence, he receives only 75% of his normal wages.

How Are Wages Determined in the Soviet World?

By the state.

The government makes an allocation for wages, industry by industry, in the five-year plan. Administrative and managerial personnel and workers are bound by the allocation.

Piece rates prevail as the method of paying labor in the Soviet world. This method, against which labor in the free world has long struggled as unjust, enables the Soviet state continually to speed up production. As productivity is increased, piece rates are lowered. "The reduction of pay rates," said the Central Committee of the Soviet Communist Party in 1947, "is an indispensable condition for the reduction of production costs."

Do Workers in the Soviet World Have the Right to Collective Bargaining?

Collective bargaining is used by the state to achieve increased productivity, speed up the workers, improve labor discipline, safety conditions, and recreational facilities. Wages, hours, and other matters of vital concern to workers are excluded from the scope of collective agreements. In the sense in which collective bargaining is understood in the free world, as a means of determining the rates and conditions of work, it is non-existent in the Soviet world.

Do Workers in the Soviet World Have the Right to Strike?

The law in the Soviet world does not forbid strikes, but the secret police do. Strikes are virtually unknown in the U.S.S.R. They are suppressed by force in the satellite states.

Do Labor Unions Exist in the Soviet World?

Organizations called labor unions are a prominent feature of industrial relations in the Soviet world. The membership of these unions is estimated at considerably more than fifty million, which is more than the number of unionists in the free world.

In name and structure, these unions are like the unions outside the Soviet orbit. In function, however, they are not voluntary organizations of workers dedicated to the improvement of the position of their members, as are the unions in the free world.

In theory, membership in unions in the Soviet world is voluntary. But the disadvantages of non-membership are so marked as to constitute an overwhelming incentive for joining. Membership in the U.S.S.R. is as high as 90% of those eligible for membership. Slave laborers are ineligible.

The Soviets believe that a union movement free to act in behalf of its members' interests is incompatible with economic planning. In addition to insuring labor discipline and increasing productivity, they also act as direct government agents in the administration of social insurance benefits, "carry out control over the condition of labor safeguards and safety techniques, negotiate collective agreements with the administration of enterprises, and perform other prescribed tasks."

The unions in the Soviet world are run by the communist party. All leading positions in these unions are held by communists, and units of the communist party function in all union bodies. Unions in the Soviet world are instruments of the state for the enslavement of the workers.

How Did Slave Labor Originate in the U.S.S.R.?

Slave labor in the Soviet Union developed from the institution of correctional labor, established after the revolution for the avowed purpose of the social rehabilitation of criminals and class enemies.

It developed in consequence of two principal factors.

One was the need, as a result of the high cost of production and low level of productivity in industry under the five-year plans, of finding a way of reducing the overall cost of production in the Soviet economy.

The second factor was the availability of a large potential labor force, created by the forcible deportation in the early 1930s of millions of peasants who resisted collectivization.

Thereafter, slave labor assumed increasingly large proportions. The supply of slave laborers was replenished and enlarged by political offenders, their relatives, persons caught up for various reasons in the periodic purges, peasants who resisted government policies, "politically unreliable" national-minority population groups, and prisoners of war.

At one time, there were up to 20,000,000 human beings in the slave labor camps, which were operated by the MVD.

The entire production of slave labor was planned, as part of the totally planned economy of the entire country. Slave labor was predominantly used in the construction of the U.S.S.R.'s atomic program, in the mining of gold and other metals, in transportation and construction of railroads, highways and defense works.

Slave laborers were not paid. They lived and worked in camps surrounded by barbed wire and patrolled by the

MVD, under literally inhuman conditions. Thousands of affidavits, memoirs and reports by former slave laborers who escaped or were fortunate enough to be released testify to the vast extent and brutality of the system.

Since Stalin's death, a measure of rationality has been introduced into the whole system. Though the camps and forced labor and secret police remain, conditions of life and work are not as bestial ast hey were. There may be no more than one million forced laborers there today, mostly political prisoners.

How Do Communism and Fascism Differ?

Soviet communism and fascism are forms of totalitarianism, the antithesis of democracy. In many respects they are identical; in others, they are poles apart.

The principal points of identity are the absolute power of the state over all economic, political, social, and cultural activities; the complete subordination of the individual to the state; the abolition of civil rights and individual liberty; regimentation and terrorization of the population; and slave labor.

The main differences are found in the economic bases and ideologies of the two systems. Under fascism, the economy is organized on the basis of private property. Under communism, the means of production, exchange and distribution are national property. Fascist ideology is, in the main, a frank glorification of nationalist supremacy and aggressive power. Communist ideology is a deceitful and deceiving perversion of the ideals of "World Brotherhood" and "Sharing."

Bibliography

Bergson, Abram
SOVIET ECONOMIC GROWTH, Row-Peterson, 1953.
A comprehensive economic history of the Soviet Union.
SOVIET NATIONAL INCOME AND PRODUCT

1940-48, Columbia University Press, 1954.

A detailed statistical investigation of the Sovie economy.

Dallin and Nikolaevsky
FORCED LABOR IN SOVIET RUSSIA, Yale University Press, 1947.

A comprehensive survey of Russian slave labor

Galenson, Walter
LABOR PRODUCTIVITY IN SOVIET AND AMERICAN INDUSTRY, Columbia University Press 1955.

A comparative analysis.

Gliksman, Jerzy
TELL THE WEST, Gresham Press, 1944.

Herling, Albert Konrad
THE SOVIET SLAVE EMPIRE, Wilfred Funk, 1941

Lipper, Elinor
ELEVEN YEARS IN SOVIET PRISON CAMPS Henry Regnery Co., 1951.

Mitrany, David
MARX AGAINST THE PEASANTS, University of North Carolina, 1951.

A study explaining the communist attitude to the peasants from the ideological point of view.

Schollmer, Joseph
VORKUTA, Holt, 1955.

The story of the slave uprisings of 1953.

Schwartz, Harry
RUSSIA'S SOVIET ECONOMY, Prentice-Hall, 1954.

A full account of Soviet economic policies up to the present.

Schwarz, Solomon
LABOR IN THE SOVIET UNION, Praeger, 1952.

An authoritative study of work in Soviet Russia.

United States Congress, Joint Economic Committee
SOVIET ECONOMIC GROWTH: A COMPARISON WITH THE UNITED STATES, 1957.

85th Congress, 1st Session, Prepared by the Legislative Reference Service of the Library of Congress.

Chapter 4

Communist China

What Is Maoism?

MAOISM IS the strategic doctrine developed by the top Chinese communist leader, Mao Tse-tung, for communist conquest of power in China, which now serves as a model of communist strategy and tactics for colonial and ex-colonial countries in Asia and Africa.

Because this doctrine addresses itself to the problem of achieving power in underdeveloped, non-industrialized countries and therefore is based on a peasant rather than proletarian movement, some observers have believed that it represents a Marxist "heresy," or a fundamental divergence from Lenin's and Stalin's teachings. Actually, Mao's political record over the past forty years reveals the most rigid adherence to Moscow's "party line" at least until Stalin's death; since then, Peking has consistently adhered to the doctrine of the U.S.S.R.'s supremacy in the communist world; and Mao's teachings are unmistakable applications of Lenin's and Stalin's views on how to gain power in backward peasant countries.

How Is Communist China Ruled?

Since 1949, when the "People's Republic of China" was established, mainland China has been ruled by a ruthless communist dictatorship which differs in no essential respect from the regime of total terror created by Stalin in the Soviet Union. The Chinese Communist Party, which has the same structure as all other communist parties, quickly established through the use of military force, police terror and massive propaganda a regime which some observers believe actually outdoes Stalin at his worst in the imposition of monolithic party dictatorship and coercion.

What Are Communist China's Economic Goals?

The Chinese communists set themselves the task, from the beginning of their regime, of making China a mighty military and industrial country. They have done this in ways very similar to those used by Stalin in the U.S.S.R. after 1928—by forcing the pace of heavy industrialization, paid for by a sweated peasantry and a population deprived of opportunities for consumption.

Just as did the Soviet Union, Communist China has undertaken this program through a series of five-year plans, the first of which covered the years 1953-57 and the second of which projects industrial advances from 1958 to 1962.

There is no doubt that heavy industrial production has soared in Communist China. At the same time, as the result of tight controls on consumption (through the manipulation of distribution, price fixing, heavy taxation, etc.) and de-emphasis of production of consumer goods, consumption in China has dropped to a lower level than ever in its modern history.

How Did Communist China Make Its Agrarian Revolution?

The vast majority of China's 650,000,000 people are peasants—fully 100,000,000 peasant families. Their fate is decisive for China's future.

In 1950, just a few months after the communists attained power, all farm land was distributed. The truly big landlords, few in number, were dispossessed, and the land distributed to peasants. Owners of small and middle-sized holdings were left in possession of their fields.

But just a few months later, still in 1950, through massive waves of mob demonstrations, lynch trials and murders, all but the tiniest parcels of land were confiscated by the state. The land distribution proceeded in such a way that the masses of peasants held even smaller land tracts than they had had before. In the next few years, tremendous propaganda and social pressures, combined with confiscatory tax policies, led increasing numbers of peasants to give up their land to the state.

In 1955, a further change of policy occurred, still moving in the ultimate direction of total collectivization of the land. A huge chain of "cooperatives" was established on semi-collectivized state farms. Peasants worked the land co-operatively and were then paid wages for their labor.

In 1957 the penultimate stage of the agrarian revolution was reached, with the complete forced collectivization of the land and the elimination of even the smallest private ownership of land. This was a stage comparable to that achieved in the U.S.S.R. during the Stalin era.

In the short space of a few months during 1958, the final stage was reached with the establishment of the communes.

What Are the Communes?

The communes represent a total revolution of family life and economics on the farms of China. They are an attempt to introduce military concepts into farming.

China's 100,000,000 peasant families have been completely broken up through the establishment of the communes. Families do not live together; children are completely separated from their parents, so that after school hours they eat, play and sleep (and work when they are of age) with their own groups. The men and women eat in separate mess dining halls constructed for each commune.

The communes vary in size from a few thousands of people to many thousands, depending on the nature of the work to which the inhabitants are assigned. In any case, this type of group organization, under para-military discipline, permits the greater coordination of large numbers of people for work projects.

The effect of the communes is essentially to break up the traditionally strong Chinese family unit, not only to facilitate more controlled and more disciplined work organization, but also to destroy the one potent institution that stood in the way of total party and state *gleichschal-*

tung (forced deprivation of individuality in the interest of total social conformity dictated from above) of the population.

What Has Happened to China's Agriculture?

In 1960 and especially in 1961, the Chinese people were in the midst of the most killing famine in centuries. This was partly the result of disastrous weather for two years running—but largely of the even more disastrous mis-planning associated with the communes. Even under the worst conditions of pre-revolutionary China, the peasants had more to eat than now. Deprived of the individuality that is so precious to the Chinese, deprived of even the minimal rations needed to sustain life, a great many Chinese peasants have either fled the countryside, or sought illegally to withhold the produce demanded of them by the regime. Untold hundreds of thousands have died of starvation, disease and overwork. The system of communes has broken down as a result. The Chinese Communist authorities have virtually admitted as much in their publications on the food crisis, though this has been done by indirection. A more overt admission has emerged from their desperate expenditure of hundreds of millions of dollars in scarce gold and U. S. currency in a drive to purchase huge quantities of grain from Canada and other Western surplus producers. Ironically, the U.S.S.R. has extended little enough aid in its ally's great crisis.

How Do the Chinese Communists Employ Terror?

The Chinese communists have added to the lessons they learned from Stalin's terror system the refinements of Chinese mental and physical torture. The secret police system extends down to every street and every dwelling. Wholesale mutual spying and public denunciation are the rule.

There have been four major periods of state-supervised terror since the communists came to power. The first was known as the "Counter-Revolutionary Suppression Campaign" which was waged in 1950 and early 1951. The second was called the "Three Anti Movement" directed at rooting out actual, alleged or even potential corruption, waste and bureaucratism; this campaign was waged in 1951. The third, the "Five Anti Movement," was directed, during the latter part of 1951 and 1952, against tax evasion, theft of government property, theft of state economic secrets, fraud and bribery.

In the course of these campaigns, conducted at an incredibly high pitch of intensity of terror and propaganda, literally millions of Chinese were killed and millions more deported to slave labor in the far reaches of China.

Those who survived with lighter penalties were considered to be successful products of what the Chinese communists have called "brain-washing."

What Is Brain-Washing?

Though the term is uniquely Chinese communist, the process is not original with Mao's Party and regime. It is actually a more outspoken version of the standard practice of all communist parties, in and out of power, when they conduct sessions of what they call "criticism and self-criticism."

Whether it is done publicly and before great crowds, as is frequently the case in China, or in the privacy of a secret party meeting, the procedure is very much the same. An individual who has fallen suspect of some alleged crime is brought before his party peers, or his neighbors, and subjected to a microscopic examination of his errors or crimes. After a severe enough mental flaying, which may continue over considerable time and more than one meeting, the accused then rises to acknowledge the correctness of the accusations, to outdo his accusers in denunciation of himself, and to promise repentance. If his self-denunciation is accepted—that is, if the authorities have predetermined that the accused is not to be put in prison, deported to slave labor or executed—he is placed on probation for a period, to demonstrate the effectiveness of the brain-washing process.

What Were "The One Hundred Flowers"?

By the spring of 1957, Mao evidently considered that the party and regime were sufficiently impervious to any resistance to allow for an extremely limited "liberalization" of the regime's rigorous control of thought and expression. In April, then, Mao made a speech in which he magnanimously proposed that the communist garden need not produce only one flower: "Let A Hundred Flowers Bloom!" he declared; the communist flower was big and sturdy enough to withstand any competition.

For six weeks the lid was off, and the steam of resentments, bitterness and frustration began to escape. It was chiefly the intellectuals, the writers, the academicians and the students who took advantage of what they supposed was a new-found right to express criticisms and to call for more rights and a generally more relaxed atmosphere. At the end of six weeks the lid was suddenly clamped down again as tightly as ever. The One Hundred Flowers began to have their heads chopped off.

All the writers and teachers and others who had expressed mild criticisms were subjected to the full process of brain-washing. Without exception they were forced to repudiate their statements, and in many cases were sentenced to penal labor or worse. In a number of cities, university student outbreaks were bloodily suppressed. Since May, 1957, no word of dissonance has been heard.

It is conceivable that Mao really believed that, in relaxing the rigors of the regime, he would encounter little outspoken criticism, and that he and his colleagues were stupefied by the extent and scale of the criticism which burst forth, and so felt it indispensable to return to the old repression.

It is at least as likely that the "Hundred Flowers" period was deliberately planned to evoke the criticism so as to lead to the discovery and liquidation of the "malcontents."

What Is the Status of Sino-Soviet Relations?

It is extremely difficult to gauge these relations accurately, since both regimes are not given to allowing open inspection of their policies. What does seem clear is that the Chinese communists are in a considerably more "revolutionary" and intransigent mood than the leadership of the U.S.S.R., that the Chinese freely concede the primacy of the Kremlin in the international movement, but that they consider themselves the first among the junior partners. They acknowledge the ideological supremacy of Moscow and proclaim the industrial achievements of the U.S.S.R. as examples to be followed by their own people. And the Soviet Union, for its part, has made China the recipient of its largest grants of economic and military aid, an increasing share of its trade; has poured hundreds of millions of rubles into China and sent scores of thousands of technicians and economic and military experts there.

That there have been conflicts between the two ruling hierarchies seems beyond doubt. Potentially there may be growing conflict in the future. But the two parties and governments have given no outward sign of encouragement to the belief that a wedge can be driven between them through outside pressures. All the evidence points to a protracted period of a solid phalanx vis-à-vis the rest of the world.

What Is China's Role in Asia?

In recent years, China has made increasingly larger claims for dominancy in Asia. Its active support, with men and arms, of communist aggressions in Korea and Indo-China reflects these aspirations, as does its outright annexation of Tibet in 1950. In Malaya, Thailand, Laos, Indonesia and other parts of South and Southeast Asia, the Chinese communists have, with the help of some elements among the colonies of overseas Chinese in those areas, built very active communist outposts.

Why Is Tibet Called "Asia's Hungary"?

Ever since the Chinese annexation of Tibet in 1950, the people of Tibet carried on overt and covert resistance. They strenuously objected, in the first place, to foreign

[Chinese] domination; they resented the communist efforts to destroy their religious institutions and practices, which are a variant of Buddhism; and they refused to accept the forcible break-up of their traditional tribal form of social and economic life. The resistance took its most overt form in the activities of Tibetan tribal guerillas against Chinese communist military formations, railroads, highways and other strategic points held or built by the Chinese.

This bloody struggle continued from 1950 to 1954, when India's Prime Minister Nehru gained the acquiescence of Tibet's temporal-religious ruler, the Dalai Lama, to China's suzerainty over Tibet on the basis of an agreement Nehru made with Chinese Premier Chou En-lai. The agreement incorporated the five points of peaceful co-existence among states known in India and throughout much of Asia as "Panch Shila." But despite this agreement, the Chinese continued to behave as brutal conquerors in Tibet.

The struggle came to a head in March, 1959, when the people of Lhasa, Tibet's capital city, rose against the oppressors in the belief that they planned the deposition and imprisonment of the Dalai Lama. Secretly, and in the dead of night, the Dalai Lama escaped from his communist-patrolled palace and made his way through a tortuous route over the Himalayas into refuge and asylum in India. In Lhasa and throughout Tibet, in subsequent weeks and months, the Chinese communists carried out bloody repressions at least comparable to the Soviet suppression of the Hungarian Revolution of 1956. Hundreds of thousands of Tibetans have been slaughtered, imprisoned, or deported to forced labor in China, and thousands of Chinese are steadily being brought to Tibet to inhabit a country increasingly depopulated of its natives. The whole process has ramifications of genocide.

Bibliography

Berger, Carl
THE KOREA KNOT, University of Pennsylvania Press, 1957.
An account of the background of the Korean War.

Feis, Herbert
THE CHINA TANGLE, Princeton University Press, 1952.
A heavily documented American view of the Chinese situation.

Hudson, G. F.; Lowenthal, Richard; MacFarquhar, Roderick
THE SINO-SOVIET DISPUTE, Praeger, 1961.
Authoritative analysis and documentation on one of the burning issues of the day.

Hunter, Edward
BRAIN-WASHING IN RED CHINA, Vanguard, 1953.
A study of the calculated destruction of men's minds.

Levi, Werner
MODERN CHINA'S FOREIGN POLICY, University of Minnesota Press, 1953.
China's foreign policy with special emphasis on its activities in South and Southeast Asia.

Lifton, Robert Jay
THOUGHT REFORM AND THE PSYCHOLOGY OF TOTALISM, Norton, 1961.
The political-psychological significance and impact of brain-washing in Communist China—a professional analysis based on numerous, dramatic case studies.

Moraes, Frank
THE REVOLT IN TIBET, Macmillan, 1960.
Provides the historical background for the revolt, and describes Asia's revulsion against China's brutality.

Tang, Peter
COMMUNIST CHINA TODAY, Praeger, 1960 (revised edition).
> The best up-to-date study.

Vatcher, William H., Jr.
PANMUNJOM, Praeger, 1958.
> The detailed story of the Korean military armistice negotiations.

Walker, Richard L.
CHINA UNDER COMMUNISM, Yale University Press, 1955.
> One of the best books on the subject.

Walker, Richard L. (editor)
LETTERS FROM THE COMMUNES, New Leader magazine special supplement, June 15, 1959.
HUNGER IN CHINA, New Leader magazine special supplement, May 10, 1960.
> In these two pamphlets the editor has compiled a valuable, revealing account of Chinese peasant life, on the basis of letters sent from the mainland to relatives living abroad.